177 MENTAL TOUGHNESS SECRETS OF THE WORLD CLASS

The Thought Processes, Habits And Philosophies Of The Great Ones

THIRD EDITION

Steve Siebold

177 Mental Toughness Secrets
of the World Class

The Thought Processes, Habits And Philosophies Of The Great Ones

Steve Siebold

Published by London House
www.londonhousepress.com

Ordering Information
To order additional copies,
visit mentaltoughnesssecrets.com
or call 561-733-9078

ISBN: 978-0-9755003-5-4

Credits

Editor: Gina Carroll
www.inkwithimpact.com

3rd Edition book design by Sandra Larson
www.SandraLarsonDesign.com

Dedication

This book is dedicated to the three most important people in my life, for their never-ending love, support and encouragement in the realization of my goals and dreams.

Dawn Andrews Siebold, my beautiful, loving wife of almost 20 years. You are my soul mate and best friend. I feel best about me when I'm with you. We've come a long way since sub-man. I love you.

Walter and Dolores Siebold, my parents, for being the most loving and supporting parents any kid could ask for. Thanks for everything you've done for me. I love you.

Acknowledgements

To my late business partner and best friend, the great **Bill Gove**, for everything you taught me and all the fun we had together building Gove Siebold Group. We will meet again, Spider. I miss you.

To **Ada Gove**, for loving and taking care of Bill for all those years, and for always supporting our work at Gove Siebold Group. Bill lived a longer, healthier and richer life because of you.

To **Larry Wilson**, for being a great friend and mentor, and for showing me how the system works.

To **Bob Proctor**, for promoting Gove Siebold Group tirelessly over the years. For always pushing me to think big.

To **John R. Spannuth**, for introducing me to Bill Gove, and for always encouraging me every step of the way. There would be no Gove Siebold Group without you.

To **Keith Harrell**, for your friendship, guidance and endless referrals.

To **Lou Wood**, for your friendship, and for your ongoing feedback during the mental toughness process. A speaker could never have a better client. A person could never have a better friend.

To all of the members of Gove Siebold Group's National Board of Advisors: **Dr. Tony Alessandra, Bill Brooks, Jim Cathcart, Dave Yoho, Dr. Jim Tunney, Mark Victor Hansen, Randy Gage, Patricia Fripp, Larry Wilson, Nido Qubein, Brian Tracy, Bob Proctor, Ray Pelletier.** For all of your advice and guidance over the years.

To **Jay Travis** and **Christy Travis Hey**, for being the example of what's possible as adults when you begin the mental toughness process as children.

To **Magic Sammy Lankford**, for being a great friend and mentor when I needed you most.

To **Brian Lee Allen**, the original great one, for helping me find my way home.

Foreword

It's important to understand that the author of this book, Steve Siebold, is not an ordinary coach, but a world-class Mental Toughness Coach. As you ponder whether or not this book is for you, think about your life. How well are you performing in the areas of your life you deem to be most important? Are you thriving or just surviving? Are you at the top of your game or sitting on the bench, watching others play, wishing you could be the star performer?

No matter how you've answered these questions, you're going to want to read this book. Why? You already know that good performance coaching is like eating healthy food. What you eat influences your energy and your body's performance. So eating healthy food just makes good sense.

But what controls how well you perform? What you think controls how you perform -- pure cause and effect. Your thinking is the cause. Your performance is the effect. So thinking the right thoughts (and acting on them) makes great sense. In fact, it makes Performance Champions. And a steady diet of "high-performance thought food" is contained in *177 Mental Toughness Secrets of the World Class*. It's your recipe for a great life, the "thought food" of champions.

Oh, did I mention that you, too, are a coach? You are the one who chooses your thought food. You're the one who swallows your thought food. And, you're the only one who is accountable for what you swallow (think). For better or worse, you are your own head coach, the coach of what thoughts are in your head.

But don't despair, Steve is here to save the day. Steve is my good friend and your primary assistant coach. He's here to assist you in making the best choices possible -- the thoughts you feed your brain. He does this by studying the thought diets of the highest performers in a variety of fields. No surprise, the best of the best feed their brains similar thought foods. This book shares this food with you.

Steve makes it easy and convenient for you to say, "I'll have what the champion performers are having." If you want to Be like a champion, you've got to Think like a champion.

Come on coach, start the Mental Toughness diet now!

Start today Playing to Win the Great Game of Your Life. There's a champion performer inside you just waiting to Get in the Game and lead a life really worthy of living.

Larry Wilson
Founder
Wilson Learning
Co-author of *Play to Win,*
Choosing growth over fear in work and in life and author of
the personal growth process, *The Great Game of Life.*

Introduction

I have had the privilege of competing against, coaching, being coached by and observing world-class performers since I was six years old. As a junior tennis player competing throughout the United States from ages 7-18, I became fascinated with what it takes to become a champion. My dream was to be ranked among the Top 10 players in the world, but I fell short. At my best, I hovered around the Top 500 in the world, and that's as high as I could seem to reach. Deep down, I knew I had the talent to make my dream a reality, and I knew the missing link was mental. After I hung up my racquet for the last time, I became obsessed with uncovering the mental toughness secrets of champions. Starting in 1984, I spent every free moment conducting interviews with champions, reading their books and studying everything I could get my hands on about the psychology of peak performance. My friends said I was obsessed. They were right. This book is the result of my 20-year obsession.

When I started to implement the ideas in this book, my whole life changed. It wasn't overnight, but sometimes it seemed like it. There's no magic here, just practical thought processes, habits and philosophies drawn from the greatest performers in the world.

This book contains no theories. Every secret comes straight from the street of experience, either my own or that of our clients. This book is loaded with ideas you can implement immediately. Some will be familiar, and some new. All of them have the power to catapult your results, no matter how high you're flying. As a matter of fact, the people who get the most value out of our mental toughness process are the world class. They are always trying to gain an edge and get better, which is one of the reasons I think so highly of them.

I've held nothing back in this book, which means that at times you may find yourself slightly offended. This book is constantly comparing 'average people' with 'world-class people'. These terms are used to get your attention and make you ask, "Which one am I?" Of course there are no 'average people', just average performers getting average results. We are all equal as human beings. I simply use these terms in reference to performance and results.

It's been said that speakers and writers espouse wisdom on the very topic they need most. Now that you know my story, you know this is true for me. After 20 years of studying and teaching mental toughness to people throughout the United States, Canada, and 10 other countries, I can honestly tell you that many times I still think like a complete amateur, operating out of the same middle-class consciousness that I ridicule in this book. After all these years, my mental toughness growth is still a work in progress. The good news is that mental toughness is a skill that can be learned, and the tougher you get, the bigger you'll dream and the more fun you'll have.

Mental toughness is the ticket to becoming one of the great ones.

I hope you'll decide to join the club.

Steve Siebold
May 1, 2004
Mexico City, Mexico

Contents

1

The World Class Operates From Objective Reality

"Amateur performers operate from delusion, pros operate from objective reality. The great ones' habits, actions, and behaviors are totally congruent with the size and scope of their ultimate vision. That's why we call them champions."

– Steve Siebold

In 20 years of competing, coaching and working with performers from various fields, I've discovered most amateurs suffer from mild to severe delusion in relation to their efforts and competencies. In other words, most people delude themselves into thinking they are working harder then they are, and that they are more competent than they actually are. Of the five major levels of conscious awareness, (poverty, working, middle, upper, and world) my experience has been that performers at the middle-class levels of consciousness suffer the grandest delusions. The poverty level is barely surviving and living in a very harsh set of circumstances. The working class is punching a mental time clock and counting the days until retirement. They're usually not expecting much, and no one around them expects much, either. They are typically not concerned about climbing any higher. It's the middle class that is most incongruent with reality. They are operating at a high enough level to understand that higher levels exist. Although they don't expect to get there, the thought crosses their minds from time to time. Because of their low expectations, their actions are incongruent with their desires. In other words, they want to live the life of the world class, but are unwilling to pay the price. Since this reality is too harsh to bear, they delude themselves into thinking they are doing everything in their power to get ahead. Of course, they're not. They'll tell you they're putting in far more time than they are. They'll swear they are thinking about their vision all the time, but they're not. The world class is brutally honest with themselves, and they tend to look reality in the face. They err on the side of over-practicing and over-preparing. Champions know that, to ascend to the top, you must first be operating from a mindset of objective reality. Self-deception and delusion have no place in the professional performer's consciousness.

LEVELS OF AWARENESS

(Individual World View)

World-Class Consciousness — 5% of population

Upper-Class Consciousness — 10% of population

Middle-Class Consciousness — 70% of population

Working-Class Consciousness — 10% of population

Poverty-Class Consciousness — 5% of population

▶ ACTION STEP FOR TODAY

Make a commitment to check delusion at the door. Be honest and ask this critical thinking question: "Are my habits, actions and behaviors congruent with the vision I have for my life?"

▶▶▌ WORLD-CLASS RESOURCE

Get a copy of Leadership and Self-Deception, by The Arbinger Institute. This book made me reexamine my entire belief system. It's a must-have for your mental toughness library.

MIDDLE CLASS VS. WORLD CLASS

1. The Middle Class competes — the World Class creates.

2. The Middle Class avoids risk — the World Class manages risk.

3. The Middle Class lives in delusion — the World Class lives in objective reality.

4. The Middle Class loves to be comfortable — the World Class is comfortable being uncomfortable.

5. The Middle Class has a lottery mentality — the World Class has an abundance mentality.

6. The Middle Class hungers for security — the World Class doesn't believe that security exists. → entrepreneurship

7. The Middle Class sacrifices growth for safety — the World Class sacrifices safety for growth.

8. The Middle Class operates out of fear and scarcity — the World Class operates from love and abundance. → Be-to-get

9. The Middle Class focuses on having — the World Class focuses on being.

10. The Middle Class sees themselves as victims — the World Class sees themselves as responsible.

11. The Middle Class slows down — the World Class calms down.

12. The Middle Class is frustrated — the World Class is grateful.

13. The Middle Class has pipedreams — the World Class has vision.

14. The Middle Class is ego-driven — the World Class is spirit driven.

15. The Middle Class is problem oriented — the World Class is solution oriented.

16. The Middle Class thinks they know enough — the World Class is eager to learn.

17. The Middle Class chooses fear — the World Class chooses growth.

18. The Middle Class is boastful — the World Class is humble.

19. The Middle Class trades time for money — the World Class trades ideas for money.

20. The Middle Class denies their intuition — the World Class embraces their intuition. → ASM

21. The Middle Class seeks riches — the World Class seeks wealth.

believe
to
see

22. The Middle Class believes their vision only when they see it — the World Class knows they will see their vision when they believe it.

emotion

23. The Middle Class coaches through logic — the World Class coaches through emotion.

24. The Middle Class speaks the language of fear — the World Class speaks the language of love.

25. The Middle Class believes problem solving stems from knowledge — the Wold Class believes problem solving stems from will.

2

World-Class Wealth Begins With World-Class Thinking

"Wealth is the product of a man's capacity to think"

– Ayn Rand, 1905-1982, author, philosopher

If you got out of bed this morning and went to work because you wanted to, you are in control of money. If you got out of bed this morning because you had to, money is in control of you. Even in the wealthiest nation in the world, 99% of the population is being controlled by money. The effect is lack of money. The cause is thinking. Albert Einstein once said, "a problem cannot be solved at the level of consciousness in which it occurs." Knowing this, champions raise their level of consciousness by studying how the world class creates wealth. The middle class believes formal education is the answer to acquiring wealth, yet very few academics are wealthy. They seek advanced degrees and certifications and are confounded when these things don't bring them riches. While the great ones are strong advocates of higher education, they don't believe it has much to do with acquiring money. The middle class trades time for money. The world class trades ideas

good quote about sing mindset

trade ideas for money (problem solving ideas)

that solve problems for money. Money flows like water from ideas. The middle class often scorns the world class out of frustration over a lack of money, yet the answer to earning more than they can spend has been in their lap their whole lives. Ideas -- it's such a simple concept that the majority misses it. The poverty class talks about and regurgitates the past; the middle class talks about other people; and the world class talks about ideas. Professional performers know money doesn't care which direction it flows. They know the world will bend over backward to make them rich if it will help them solve their problems. About 150 years ago, Karl Marx was sure the working class, as a whole, would rise up and overcome oppression if they had a chance. What Marx didn't figure into the equation was the poverty-driven thought process of the people. Give people operating at middle-class conscious-ness a million-dollar opportunity, and they will find a way to make it back to the middle class. It is where their limited self-image tells them they belong. The difference has nothing to do with reality. It's all perception in the mind of the performer.

importance of friendship

▶ ACTION STEP FOR TODAY

Ask this critical thinking question: "At what level of monetary success do I feel most comfortable? a) poverty class b) middle class c) world class." Where you feel most comfortable reflects your self-image, and most likely, your current status. If you want to become wealthier, begin by raising your self-image by upgrad-ing the self-talk you use regarding money and finances. If all you do is chase more money, you are simply attacking the effect. The cause is how you think, and if you improve the cause, the effect will take care of itself.

not to chase after #

▶▶I WORLD-CLASS RESOURCE

Read You Were Born Rich, by Bob Proctor. This man knows more about the mind/money connection than anyone alive. I study everything he produces like a scientist.
Learn more about him at www.bobproctor.com

3

Champions Have An Immense Capacity For Sustained Concentration

"Nothing can add more power to your life than concentrating all of your energies on a limited set of targets."

– *Nido Qubein, speaker, author, philanthropist*

Champions are famous for concentrating their energy and efforts on what they want and blocking out anything or anyone who threatens that focus. While average people haphazardly pursue loosely defined goals, champions concentrate on the attainment of a singular purpose with an intensity that borders on obsession. World-class performers invest an inordinate amount of time and energy in selecting their major goals. While the masses consider making changes every New Year's Eve, the goal setting and planning process is an everyday habit of champions. When the goals are set, champions put mental blinders on and move forward with dogged persistence and ferocious tenacity. World-class performers create such an intense level of concentration to overcome challenges and achieve goals that it is the last thing they think about before they fall asleep, and the first thing that hits them when they wake up. The great ones dream about their goals so frequently that they often keep pen and paper on the nightstand so they can quickly record any ideas or solutions that come to them in the middle of the night. While average people see world-class performers' successes as a matter of intelligence or luck, champions know sustained concentration of thought and action is usually the true key to their success.

▶ **ACTION STEP FOR TODAY**

Write down the single most important goal you want to achieve in the next twelve months and make a commitment to concentrate on achieving it – no matter what it takes.

▶▶| **WORLD-CLASS RESOURCE**

Read Focal Point, by Brian Tracy. This book is required reading for all Mental Toughness University clients in corporate America.

4

Champions Are Driven By Emotional Motivators

"When a performer begins to experience physical or emotional pain in the heat of the battle, the brain, whose primary role is self preservation, asks the question: 'Why must I suffer?' The champion will answer the question with the vision they have carefully constructed, and they will continue to fight. Since the masses lack this mental clarity and have no reason to suffer, they quit as soon as the pain kicks in. Developing a world-class vision is the secret to world-class motivation."

– Steve Siebold

The masses are primarily motivated by extrinsic motivators, such as material possessions and money. The world class is motivated intrinsically, by their dreams, desires and passions. External motivation is short lived, while internal motivation is nearly impossible to exhaust until the goal is achieved. The rah-rah, jump-up-and-down motivational pep talks are fun and temporarily motivating, yet lack the real fire emotional motivators generate. World-class leaders know the secret to motivating themselves and others is discovering what they will fight for when the going gets tough. The great ones move from logic-based motivators to emotion-based motivators. They know the key to finding the true power of the individual lies in the deep recesses of the psyche. The process great leaders and coaches use is tedious, time consuming, and simple: ask questions, and don't stop until you have landed on the emotional hot buttons. World-class coaches keep digging until they hit the vein of gold – when the performer begins answering in terms of how they feel, as opposed to what they think. When they hit the vein of gold, they continue to probe until the performer reaches an emotional high point, known in performance circles as the white moment. The white moment is the strongest emotional driver of a performer. Coaches use emotional drivers to motivate and inspire performers to push far beyond their threshold of pain, to accomplish feats that, without this level of motivation, would be impossible.

What is your white moment?

▶ ACTION STEP FOR TODAY

1) Integrity, gender equality
2) Integrity
3) Integrity   nake all my
4) *Help people ~~achieve~~ live   I I tell my
   a happier life through *financial*   learned about
                          freedom   l you a lot
                          and
5) • Integrity   *Self-image*
                          liberation
   • Charity
   • Self-fulfilment   an, Ph.D.

5

The Great Ones Separate
Truth From Fact

Before you program dreams ideas as truth

"We have to live today by what truth we can get today
and be ready tomorrow to call it falsehood."
— *William James, 1842-1910, author*

While average performers tend to believe truth and fact are the same, the world class knows there is a difference. Champions use their critical thinking skills to make a clear distinction between truth and fact. Fact is reality. Truth is our perception of reality, and perceptions are subjective. One person perceives giving to charity as an expense, while another perceives it as an investment in someone else's life. The fact is that many people give to charity; whether it's an expense or an investment is a perception. Which line of thinking represents truth? Both. In the minds of individuals, perception equals truth. This subtle distinction allows the great ones to understand themselves and others at a higher level of awareness. The masses tend to operate from truth, which is often a distorted version of facts. Champions make decisions based on facts, not feelings. The world class also uses this understanding of truth and fact in their mental programming. The great ones know the conscious mind functions most effectively on fact, while the subconscious can be programmed with truth. Since the subconscious is unable to make the distinction between fact and truth, champions program their subconscious minds to believe their visions, dreams and ideas as truths. Because the subconscious doesn't have the ability to reject an idea, it accepts it as truth and begins to create behaviors that are congruent with this new "truth." The conscious mind knows this "truth" is not fact, and tension begins to build between the conscious and subconscious, creating cognitive dissonance. As a result, the two go to work to create congruency. The great ones are not only aware of the difference between truth and fact, but they also know how to use them both to get what they want.

▶ **ACTION STEP FOR TODAY**

Write down 10 things you know are fact, and rethink each by asking, "Is this really a fact, or a truth I've created from my own or others' perceptions?" For example: is it a fact that the sky is blue? Is it a fact that you are a nice person? Is it a fact that the faithful will be rewarded in heaven? You'll see how often we operate from truth, rather than fact.

6

Champions Lead Through Facilitated Introspection

"The great managers and leaders of the future will know more about their people than ever before. They'll know their emotional hot buttons as well as the essence of what makes them tick. Through facilitated introspection, these leaders will create a competitive immunity for their companies by reigniting the flame of loyalty that burns within their people."

— *Steve Siebold*

All great leaders know that the most effective form of learning is self-discovery. World-class coaches and managers believe in facilitating the introspective process, which helps people rediscover what they already know. Instead of leadership through the outdated command-and-control, do-it-or-you're-fired model, progressive managers are constantly asking their employees questions *coach through emotion*

care about how they think and feel

and taking careful note of their answers. The great ones know that most people are unaware of what makes them tick in terms of their emotional motivators. The only way to help a person discover the hidden power locked up in their psyche is through asking probing questions. Learning occurs at two levels during this introspective process. The first level is when the person digging down inside himself becomes aware of the emotions driving his behavior, and the second is the manager's awareness as it relates to which buttons to push when it's time to motivate his charge to action. Amateur coaches and managers coach primarily through logic. Professional coaches and managers coach primarily through emotion. Since human beings are primarily emotional creatures, it's obvious which method has the most power. Facilitating the introspective process in another person requires patience and time, and the great ones are willing to invest. The amateur wants instant results, but pros know this rarely occurs. The payoff for the pro comes not only in the form of increased productivity, but also in the connection created between manager and employee. Once an emotional creature is convinced that you care about what she thinks and how she feels, it sets the stage for emotional bonding to occur. Managers and leaders who lead this way lose very few of their people to rival companies because of this bond. In the age of the mind, facilitated introspection is the core process of leadership.

Facilitated Introspection

▶ **ACTION STEP FOR TODAY**

Invest 20 minutes today leading someone through the introspective process. Your first question should be: Tell me what you really want out of life more than anything else? Your goal should be to make the person comfortable enough to answer you in terms of how she feels, rather than how she thinks. Once she begins to explain her feelings, follow up with these questions:

1) What exactly do you mean by that?
2) What does that look like?
3) Why do you feel that way?
4) Tell me more about that.

5) Why is that important to you?

6) What does having that mean to you?

7

The Great Ones Know They Are Unaware

*"Everyone is operating and running their lives at
their current level of conscious awareness."*

– Carlos Marin, speaker and author

[handwritten: keep learning + becoming]

Champions have come so far in raising their level of awareness
that they realize there is always a higher level. Average people
have a world view that says being comfortable with who and
where they are in life is the key to happiness. The great ones have a
world view that says happiness is learning, growing and becoming.
School is never out for champions. The more they learn, the more
they realize how much they don't know. While average people seek
mental comfort, the world class believes mental comfort is the
death of growth. They live by this phrase: 'You're either growing
or dying; stagnation does not exist in the universe.' Like the child
who always asks "why," champions always ask questions of other
top performers in an effort to get a new take on an old idea. Their
ongoing mental growth reinforces their belief of another level of
conscious awareness that can make them more successful, more
fulfilled and happier.

▶ **ACTION STEP FOR TODAY**

Ask yourself this critical thinking question: Am I growing or
dying? If your answer is dying, make the decision today to
become more aware and begin growing.

▶▶I **WORLD-CLASS RESOURCE**

Get a copy of The Handbook to Higher Consciousness, by Ken Keyes Jr. This timeless classic will provoke you to think at a higher level.

8

Champions Develop World-Class Beliefs Long Before They Become Champions

"They can . . . because they think they can."
– *Unknown*

One of the major distinctions between average performers and champions is their belief system. Like champions, average people tend to be a product of their mental programming from childhood. People of influence, such as parents, teachers, coaches, religious leaders, and others were the primary builders and shapers of our early belief systems. In most cases, this programming is limiting because it comes from people who believe they are limited. That's why average people are saddled with a set of beliefs that are more about survival than success. Average people have been programmed to avoid pain at all costs, which promotes a 'playing not to lose' mentality. Many world-class performers were raised with these same beliefs, yet learned to reprogram themselves somewhere along the way. Champions learn how to develop empowering beliefs and invest a substantial amount of time solidifying those beliefs, mostly through their own self-talk. With guidance from coaches and mentors, champions monitor the words they use. They know reprogramming is a never-ending activity. Some people even consider this process 'positive brainwashing.' When aspiring champions learn they can program any belief they wish, and through repetitious, ongoing self-talk, build that belief into a foundation for their consciousness, it's a revelation. A world-class belief system can be created from scratch, no matter what your age, upbringing or current lot in life. A world-class belief system is a primary factor in the making of a champion, and every great performer knows it. While average people see champions as more intelligent, the champions know better. The truth is that intelligence plays a small part. Belief is the real star of the show.

THE EVOLUTION OF A BELIEF SYSTEM

Parents, teachers, coaches, ministers, friends, relatives, and other people of influence in a child's life say to the child: "This is Fact."

Child accepts elders' perception of what is fact
-- even if elder is completely wrong.

Child unconsciously ingrains these beliefs in his/her sub-conscious, and builds habits accordingly.

Child grows into an adult operating under dozens of faulty beliefs and habits, but is not consciously aware of it.

Adult operates under false and limiting beliefs and sets invisible boundaries for his/her life at an unconscious level.

▶ ACTION STEP FOR TODAY

Make a list of your most closely held beliefs, and begin the process of questioning whether they are serving you or holding you back. Question their validity. Are they relevant, or out of date? Knowing that behavior follows belief, give yourself an opportunity to discard or upgrade any beliefs that limit you.

▶▶I WORLD-CLASS RESOURCE

approval of others + conformity

Rent the movie Rudy. This true story of one man's dream to become a Notre Dame football player clearly demonstrates the power of belief. As you're watching, ask this critical thinking question: "Do I believe in myself as much as Rudy had to in order to accomplish his dream? If not, how

D watch Rudy

can I change or upgrade my belief to catapult my mental power?"

9

Champions Embrace Relativity

"The great ones are highly aware of the fact that all perceptions are based on the experience and belief of the beholder. This is the reason they surround themselves with people who think much bigger than they do. Beliefs and expectations are contagious, and champions are eager to catch as much as they can."

– *Steve Siebold*

Think bigger – have a bigger belief and expectation.

The masses measure and assign value to things based on their own perspective. The world class is much more discerning in their thought processes. They realize all things are relative. This is most apparent in their life vision. Most people typically won't invest the time to create a vision and commit it to paper, yet the few who do tend to aim low as a result of their own limited perspective and beliefs. Ask champions if their vision is big, and they are likely to respond, "Compared to what?" The great ones develop the unique ability to measure beyond their own perspective. This is one of the secrets which enables them to reach for goals and dreams far exceeding anything they have accomplished in the past. The goal, dream or vision may be big to them, but to a bigger champion with a broader perspective, it's child's play. This critical thinking skill removes the intimidation factor and raises their level of expectation. Is a million dollars a lot of money? The masses would say, "yes." The world class asks, "Compared to what?" Compared to a dollar, a million dollars is a lot of money. Compared to one hundred million dollars, it's not much at all. Don't underestimate this seemingly minute subtlety, because adopting this one simple principle could transform your perception of every aspect of your life.

▶ **ACTION STEP FOR TODAY**

Listen to how people around you measure the size and scope of things. When you hear someone placing a value on something, using their own perspective as a reference point, challenge them. For example, if someone says, "This is a huge project, Bob," reply, "Really. Compared to what?" Try this and see the reaction you get.

10

The World Class Compartmentalizes Emotions

"Nothing external to you has any power over you."
– *Ralph Waldo Emerson, 1803-1882, minister, speaker, writer*

Professional performers make the difficult look easy. They're able to manage multiple problems and maintain emotional control while solving each problem individually. Average people get bogged down in the details of every little problem and become overwhelmed quickly. Professional performers compartmentalize each problem and create a mental/emotional separation between the person and the problem. Pros don't engage in the emotional aspects of each problem; they focus on a logical solution and then put it aside so they can focus on the next challenge. In our Mental Toughness University seminar, we call this The Presidential Problem-Solving Technique. The idea: the President of the United States has multiple life-and-death decisions to make daily, and must possess the ability to place each problem in a mental box that separates it from all the other problems of the day. The ability to compartmentalize problems is a hallmark of great leaders. Champions know every problem has a logical solution (at best) or a practical strategy (at least) which can make things a little better. While amateurs get tangled in emotions, professionals are grounded in logical problem solving. Compartmentalization allows champions to work on and solve one problem at a time, without the emotions of one problem bleeding into the solutions of the others.

▶ **ACTION STEP FOR TODAY**

Commit to compartmentalizing problems by focusing exclusively on one problem at a time. Imagine you are the President of the United States. You must keep a clear, unemotional mind during the problem-solving process. The masses multitask. The great ones focus.

one thing at a time.

▶▶| **WORLD-CLASS RESOURCE**   *Step in, step out*

Read The Emotional Revolution, by Norman Rosenthal, M.D.

11

The World Class Connects To The Source Through Gratitude

Mentally detach from end results

Focus on being, rather than doing

Tap into your ATM through relaxation and gratitude

"Gratitude is the aristocrat of all of the emotions."
— *Bill Gove, 1912-2001, the father of professional speaking*

The world class is famous for using non linear thinking as a primary problem solving strategy, and nowhere is this more apparent than when it comes to heightening their creativity. While amateurs become increasingly stressed during problem solving, the great ones become more relaxed to enhance their creative ability. Champions know the ultimate creative force is located somewhere

our everyday consciousness, and they must tap this source
.ierate their best ideas. The secular sometimes refer to this
.rce as the unconscious mind. The spiritual often call it God.
, hatever label their belief warrants, few deny the power of the
source, whatever its point of origin. Champions know the fastest
way to connect to the source is through gratitude. Thoughts and
feelings of gratitude seem to elevate the performers' consciousness to a higher plane than is accessible through any other means.
Professional writers call it being connected. Athletes call it being in
the zone. Psychologists refer to it as a state of flow. No matter what
name you assign it, the experience is the same. It's a process that
begins by letting go and mentally detaching from the end result or
outcome of any task. The focus is on being, as opposed to doing.
While both amateurs and pros experience this phenomenon from
time to time, the great ones are able to access it much more often
because they are aware of the triggers that create a mental climate
conducive to this state of mind. Gratitude is the mindset of choice
when they need to awaken the giant and tap their genius.

▶ **ACTION STEP FOR TODAY**

Make a list of the ten things you are most grateful for in your
life, and review them every morning for the next seven days.
Monitor how this activity impacts your emotions.

12 *mental training ground.

Champions Know Adversity Is The Catalyst Of Mental Toughness

"If it weren't for the dark days, we wouldn't know what it is to walk in the light."

— Earl Campbell, professional football player

my daily habit of discipline

Champions believe if you remove the adversity, you remove the victory. As a result, they tend to view adversity as a challenge through which learning and growing occurs. Their world view is evident in the way they describe the adversities they face. While average people choose the path of least resistance, world-class performers operate at a higher level of awareness. They understand that stress and struggle are the key factors in becoming mentally tough. While average people watch television and hang out at happy hour, the great ones continue to push themselves mentally and physically to the point of exhaustion. Only then will you see them in rest and recovery situations. Adversity, to average people, equals pain. Adversity, to world-class performers, is their mental training ground. It's how they become mentally tough. Average people scorn adversity. Those who are world class don't welcome adversity; yet they see it as the ultimate catalyst for mental growth, as well as the contrast needed to recognize the beauty of life.

▶ ACTION STEP FOR TODAY

List the three most difficult adversities you have faced and five good things that happened to you as a result of each one. Train yourself to see the good in adversity, and your fear of future challenges will dissipate.

▶▶| **WORLD-CLASS RESOURCE**

Read Man's Search for Meaning, by Viktor Frankel. It is the true story of how one man learned to control his thoughts, feelings and attitudes as a prisoner of war. It's a classic that should be a part of every champion's library.

13

The Great Ones Do It All With Class

"There is no mat space for malcontents or dissenters. One must neither celebrate too insanely when he wins or sulk when he loses. He accepts victory professionally and humbly. He hates defeat, but makes no poor display of it."

— Dan Gable, collegiate wrestling legend

True champions have class, and they consistently conduct themselves in a manner congruent with their self-image. While amateur performers publicly gloat in their victories and agonize in their defeats, professional performers tend to keep a low profile during times of great success, and during times of failure. Another hallmark of the great ones is their humility after triumph. They tend to project themselves in the same manner whether they are winning or losing. When they win, they love to share the credit with the team, and when they lose, they assume 100 % responsibility. This high-class approach to performance opens doors which propel champions to even greater success. The great ones like to associate and do business with people who know how to handle themselves, especially in adverse situations under pressure. This is one of the primary distinctions between the upper class and the world class. The ego-driven upper class must win at any cost; the spirit-driven world class insists on following a strict code of ethics. The great ones have the character to do what's right, and they do it all with class.

▶ ACTION STEP FOR TODAY

Make a list of the five things you would like the following groups of people to say about your conduct:

1) Your family
2) Your friends
3) Your customers

Now go to work and become this person.

▶▶I WORLD-CLASS RESOURCE

To further polish your personal and professional behavior, attend a seminar from Jacqueline Whitmore, director of the Protocol School of Palm Beach. Sign up for their free newsletter by going to www.etiqetteexpert.com

14

Champions Make 'Do or Die' Commitments

"You cannot keep a committed person from success. Place stumbling blocks in his way, and he takes them for stepping-stones, and on them he will climb to greatness. Take away his money, and he makes spurs of his poverty to urge him on. The person who succeeds has a program; he fixes his course and adheres to it; he lays his plans and executes them; he goes straight to his goal. He is not pushed this side and that every time a difficulty is thrust in his way. If he can't get over it, he goes through it."

– George Gilder, author

champion= commitment

If there was ever one word that defined the champion, the word would be commitment. When everyone else is tired, exhausted and burned out from the battle, the great ones are just getting warmed up. It's not that they don't fatigue; but their commitment to their dream keeps them going. Average people think it would be nice to achieve their goals, as long as it doesn't get too uncomfortable or painful. Champions don't recognize pain, because they have made a commitment to do what it takes to win. Amateur performers make a commitment and approach it like a hobby. Professional performers make a commitment and approach it like a war, knowing they will have to endure an unknown level of suffering

(handwritten margin note: do whatever it takes to win ↓ approach like a war, not like a hobby)

(handwritten note on card:)

Commitment   congru-ent?

① Be a good mom

② Be a good wife

③ EVC in WFG

④ Sale of VHM CA to IPG

⑤ Be a generous connector and philanthropist

...ways question the ...ay whatever price ...strategy makes all ...ore about making ...an anything else, ...ves to make these ...gs you are com-...hinking question: ...ngruent with my

The World Class Is Consistently Great

*(handwritten margin note: * Habit of excellence)*

> "Plenty of men can do good work for a spurt with immediate promotion in mind, but for promotion, you want a man in whom good work has become a habit."
> – *Henry Doherty, American Industrialist*

A lot of performers are capable of outstanding performance, but the great ones all have one thing in common: consistency. Day after day, they perform at the very highest levels. The reason they are so consistent is because their actions are congruent with their thought processes. Champions usually have a very clear mental picture of what they want, why they want it, and how to move closer to their target objective. While average people are complaining about the sacrifices they have to make to be great, the champions have already made those decisions and continue to move forward. Erratic performance is the result of erratic thinking, so the first step in mental toughness training is gaining mental clarity. Champions invest an inordinate amount of time thinking, planning and clarifying their goals and targets, as well as mapping out an exact action plan for attainment. Consistency in performance is the direct result of knowing why it is necessary to perform well and the benefits that will accrue, especially when the going gets tough and the pain sets in. Consistency is also created by practice. Champions are usually thought of as the people with the most talent, and sometimes this is true. Yet champions are known to invest large blocks of time practicing their craft long after everyone else has gone home. Practice may not make perfect, but it does create consistency in performance.

▶ **ACTION STEP FOR TODAY**

To gain mental clarity and focus, create a written vision for your life. Imagine your life five to ten years in the future and list all you have done, accumulated and become during this time. Use the letter to a friend format that we use in our corporate Mental Toughness University program. Write a letter to a friend – real or imaginary – and date it from five to ten years in the future. Let your creative mind freewheel, without any thought of how you will achieve any of these things. Be sure to include as many details and as much emotion as possible. When you have a world-class vision for your life, you've taken the first step to world-class performance.

▶▶❙ **WORLD-CLASS RESOURCE**

Sign up for the Mental Toughness University one-day seminar and 12 month follow-up process. Learn more by visiting www.mentaltoughnessuniversity.com

16

Champions Understand
Logic vs. Emotion

"The arena was so loud, the emotion so great. Everybody was going crazy. I remember thinking, 'Stay with it. Don't get swept up.' The hotter it gets, the cooler you have to get. I remember thinking of one word in my mind–'miraculous.'"

– Al Michaels, sports announcer, commenting on the 1980

U.S. Olympic Hockey Team victory over the Soviet Union amateur managers, coaches and leaders tend to favor either a logic-based approach to performance or an emotion-based approach. The pros know the magic is in the mix. When it comes to strategic planning and business acumen, straight logic is essential. Emotion creates confusion when it comes to linear thought. This is why amateurs in the business world have repeated the idea that there is no place for emotion in business. Professional leaders know this is ridiculous. As you know, human beings are emotional creatures driven by emotional motivators like love, recognition, belonging, pride, values, etc. The list goes on and on. To ignore the role emotion plays in performance is to disregard the power of the fire that burns within a person's soul. The real distinction between amateur leaders and pros that amateurs motivate through logic and the great ones motivate through emotion. Logic is great for planning, but weak for motivation. Trying to inspire an emotional creature by appealing to their sense of logic is amateur at best, and stupid at worst. In twenty years of studying and working with leaders, only a small percentage has really understood this in the business world. In the world of professional sports, it's a different story. Many top coaches use emotional motivation brilliantly.

The best example may be Herb Brooks, who motivated the U.S. Olympic Hockey team in 1980 to pull one of the greatest upsets in history. Emotional motivation has the power to drive a team beyond what they actually believe is possible. The sheer force of the collective emotion is so overwhelming that it mentally elevates the consciousness of the individual performers, which enables them to tap into a higher level of intelligence. The secular philosophy is that the performers are able to access more of their brain when they are operating in this altered state of consciousness. The spiritual philosophy says that performers have raised their rate of vibration to the same frequency as the force that created the universe. While champions' belief in the source of this power varies, they all know that the process begins with emotional motivation.

▶ ACTION STEP FOR TODAY

Watch the movie Miracle. This film is the story of the 1980 U.S. Olympic hockey team victory over the Soviet Union. Notice how coach Herb Brooks uses emotion to mold a group of individuals into a world-class team.

* Logic for planning
* Emotion for motivation

17

Champions Are Willing To
Suspend Their Disbelief

* Be open-minded (handwritten)

"When presented with a new idea, check your ego at the
door and suspend your disbelief. Your ability to open
your mind and consider new ideas without fear will
propel you to the top faster than anything else."
— *Bill Gove, 1912-2001, the father of professional speaking*

The world class is the most open-minded group of people you
will ever meet, which is one of the reasons for their tremendous success. While amateur thinkers are convinced they have figured out how the world works, champions are not so sure, and
are open to new ways of looking at old problems. In other words,
champions are willing to suspend their disbelief until they evaluate
the facts. The great ones are ready to change at a moment's notice
if they are convinced something can be done faster, cheaper or
better. A great example is in the network marketing profession,
where sales reps recruit other sales reps and are compensated
with an override on their recruit's volume. Strong companies with
quality products and services are able to grow at an alarmingly
accelerated rate with this reproductive recruiting model. Network
marketing has single handedly changed the face of distribution
for the better, yet has still not been fully embraced by amateur
thinkers who insist on clinging to the past. Franchising faced
the same scorn years ago from amateurs who didn't understand
it and refused to open their minds to innovation and progress.
The great ones capitalized on that concept and made history with
companies like McDonald's, Radio Shack and Blockbuster Video,
while the masses took years to accept this brilliant business idea as

Example NM (handwritten)

legitimate. The heart of the champions' open-minded attitude is in their spirit-based consciousness, which is a mindset devoid of the need to hold on to the past. Most new ideas with the power to revolutionize people's lives never make it past the amateurs' ego, which is rooted in fear of the unknown and marked by pre-judgment, pretense and frustration. While the masses are dying from mental stagnation, the pros grow healthier everyday by entertaining thoughts of abundance and keeping their fertile minds open to life and successful living.

▶ **ACTION STEP FOR TODAY**

Think back to the last time someone approached you with a new idea that you were quick to dismiss, and give it a second chance. Suspend your disbelief, open your mind and give it careful consideration. What have you got to lose?

18

The World Class Is Ferociously Cooperative

"You can employ men and hire hands to work for you, but you must win their hearts to have them work with you."
– *William Boetcker,*

1873-1962, Presbyterian minister, success lecturer

Professional performers are the most cooperative people in the world, because they know it takes a team to achieve anything worthwhile. Their cooperation stems from their desire to win. They know they cannot do it alone. Amateurs tend to be more ego involved and prefer to act as lone wolves, so they can boast they are self-made. Champions don't need to take all of the credit, and as a rule, enjoy sharing the accolades with their team. Champions believe the whole is greater than the sum of the parts when it comes to achievement. These people have a tremendous ability to persuade others to join forces with them, and work in a spirit of ferocious cooperation. Achievement has less to do with stroking their egos and more to do with personal growth and development – not just their own, but also that of the team. Champions get as big a kick from watching a team member grow in the process of achieving the goal as they do in actually achieving the goal. They realize the true value of achievement is as a catalyst for growth. Generally speaking, the more cooperative the champion, the more successful they tend to be. The great individual is no match for the great team.

▶ ACTION STEP FOR TODAY

Rate yourself on your level of cooperation. In your opinion, you are:

1 - Very cooperative with others
2 - Somewhat cooperative
3 - Not very cooperative
4 - Not cooperative at all

If you rate a 2, 3, or 4, ask yourself if you are allowing your ego to get in the way. If the answer is yes, check your ego at the door and become a team player.

19

Champions Are Curious

> "Curiosity is one of the most permanent and certain
> characteristics of a vigorous intellect."
> – Samuel Johnson, 1709-1784, writer

The great ones are always curious, because they are always looking for an edge. At the root of their curiosity is the belief

[handwritten margin notes: "- ask Qs", "eager to learn", "- curiosity", "mth beginner - open to new ideas"]

that one new idea, or one new twist on an old idea, could launch them to the next level. While average people tend to take things at face value, world-class performers are curious to know how and why something works in an effort to make new distinctions that may benefit them. Champions have a childlike curiosity, and tend to approach the world with a mindset that says, "teach me." Their world view tells them there is much more to learn in even the simplest aspects of life. The more they know, the more they realize how much they don't know about anything, including their own expertise. They approach their work with the mindset of a beginner — eager to learn and open to new ideas. Professional performers are curious to see how beginners view their performance field, and want to see if anything can be learned from people who are seeing what they do for the first time. Champions are masters at learning from other people's experiences because they are always asking questions. Their curiosity accelerates their growth through lessons learned vicariously.

▶ ACTION STEP FOR TODAY

The next time you are socializing with friends or associates, see how many questions you can ask each about what they do and why they do it. Get as many details as possible. Most people are full of great suggestions for solving problems, yet no one asks for their opinion. Your curiosity, combined with a beginner's mindset, may yield unexpected solutions you can implement immediately.

20

The Great Ones Possess Supreme Confidence

"I felt like I could score at will."
— Jack Maitland, 1970 Super Bowl champion
fullback, speaking of his college football career

Another great word to distinguish world-class performers from average people is confidence. Some people are raised by confidence-building parents, teachers and coaches, yet they are in the minority. Most champions realized they were responsible for developing their own confidence at some point, and programmed themselves through a series of ongoing techniques. These programming strategies might include mental imagery and visualization techniques, meditation, sports, martial arts, learning a new language or musical instrument, or losing weight and going on an exercise regimen. All these strategies contribute to boosting self-confidence, but the two fastest, most powerful ways to skyrocket self-confidence I've ever seen are:

1) Changing the language you use when you talk to yourself and others. Positive self-talk can literally change your life in ninety days, if you really stick to it. You can reprogram your entire belief system just by changing the words you use when you talk to yourself. I've read volumes of books on this subject, and the best one is called What to Say When You Talk to Yourself, by Shad Helmstetter, Ph.D. This book is written in simple language and explains how the change process works.

2) Learning to be a proficient and entertaining public speaker. When you can stand in front of a group of people and communicate effectively, it catapults your confidence into the stratosphere. Most world-class business people are strong speakers.

▶ **ACTION STEP FOR TODAY**

Ask your three closest friends this question: On a scale of 1 to 7, 7 being most confident, how much confidence do I project? This will give you an idea of how the world is responding to you.

▶ **WORLD-CLASS RESOURCE**

To upgrade the quality of your self-talk, purchase Shad Helmstetter's book, What to Say When You Talk to Yourself. I read this book in 1986 and it changed my life. I would also recommend that you get a free subscription to 'The Greatest Things Ever Said about Public Speaking,' a free weekly e-mail. To sign up, go to www.publicspeakersblog.com

21

Champions Evolve From Competing to Creating

> "Creative people rarely need to be motivated--they have their own inner drive that refuses to be bored. They refuse to be complacent. They live on the edge, which is precisely what is needed to be successful and remain successful."
>
> *— Donald Trump, real estate developer*

Average performers live their lives in first gear, resisting change and avoiding risk. The masses have the same talent and opportunity as the world class; yet choose to play it safe to avoid the pain of failure and the agony of (temporary) defeat. At Mental Toughness University, we have a scale called The Five Levels of Mental Toughness, which is a tool to help people determine at what level they are performing. The first level is called Playing Not to Lose, which is doing just enough to avoid getting fired. The next level up is Playing To Cruise, which is mentally cruising through the job without really engaging in any serious thought. The next level is Playing to Improve, which is when performers begin to actively engage their thoughts and feelings in the task at hand, attempting to get better. The level above this is Playing To Compete, which is when performers begin to believe they are capable of beating out their competition and being the best. This level is primarily ego-driven where winning is the main objective. Performers operating at this level often become very successful and powerful, but are sometimes left with hollow feelings of "Is this all there is?" The highest level is Playing to Win, which occurs when the performer moves from competition to creation, where the primary goal is to be the best they can be. Knowing that creativity and fear cannot co-exist, these people are competing only with themselves with the objective of being better today than they were yesterday. The Playing to Win philosophy is rooted in a spirit-based consciousness operating from thoughts of love and abundance. Fear and scarcity have no place at this level of thinking. These performers are fearlessly seeking what Dr. Abraham Maslow referred to as Self-Actualization, or becoming all that one has the potential to become. The most powerful belief performers operating at this level possess is that they cannot fail; they can only learn and grow. With their potential in front and their fear behind them, champions are able to move beyond the boundaries of competition and create what the masses believe is impossible.

▶ ACTION STEP FOR TODAY

Examine the 5 Levels of Mental Toughness and identify the level you inhabit most often in performance situations. Make a commitment to spend as much time at the Playing To Win level as possible.

5 LEVELS OF MENTAL TOUGHNESS

PLAYING TO WIN - "I cannot fail, I can only learn and grow. The only person I'm competing with is myself. I no longer feel fear, because it's impossible for me to lose. I feel so grateful just to have an opportunity to be the best I can be. I see my performance as the primary catalyst of my self-actualization. I don't have to be who I've always been. I learn and I grow; that's how I win. *An event awakens the performer and triggers inner wisdom. Performer starts to see his/her performance as a game in which there is no way to lose. Performer is driven by spirit instead of ego, devoid of pretense, and totally focused. Fear does not exist at this level, only love.*

PLAYING TO COMPETE - "I think I can be the best!" *New success expands the belief system. Performer is powerful, but still driven by ego gratification.*

PLAYING TO IMPROVE - "Maybe I can accomplish more than I thought. Maybe I'm better than I think I am." *Belief-altering event occurs triggering a new thought process.*

PLAYING TO CRUISE - "As long as I continue to perform, I can cruise."

PLAYING NOT TO LOSE - "I better perform or I'll be in trouble."

22

Champions Remember Their Roots

"We usually think of advice as something that someone tells us, but I learned my most valuable lessons in life by example, by watching people around me both when I was growing up and when I was trying to stay true, in my business career, to the values they taught me. Yet, if there is one piece of advice that has been important to me, it is "Always remember where you came from."
— *John J. Mack, Co-CEO, Credit Suisse Group*

Professional performers start out as amateurs, just like everyone else, and they never forget it. While the masses see this as humility, the great ones see it as strategy. They know the lessons they learned on Main Street are just as valuable on Wall Street. The great ones never forget where they came from. This strategy keeps them grounded and enables them to relate to middle-class performers struggling to go pro. This empathy for amateurs makes them tremendous managers, coaches and leaders. Champions often cultivate this habit by staying connected to people who helped lift them to the top, and by giving back to the community in which they were raised. The world class is always reaching for the stars while keeping their feet on the ground. This high level of consciousness is revealed in the language they use in conversation. You'll hear them speak about the gratitude they feel for all of the people who contributed to their success and fulfillment. While the masses are still angry over the injustices of their past, the champions are grateful and giving back. As a result of this abundance-based mindset, their blessings are multiplied many times over. The great ones know success is a self-fulfilling prophecy, and remembering their roots reminds them of not only where they came from, but also what it took to get them where they are now. Revisiting their climb to the top reinforces their belief in themselves and gives them even more confidence to move ahead in the present and future. This is one of the ways champions build the psychological momentum necessary to propel them from success to success.

▶ ACTION STEP FOR TODAY

Invest ten minutes today remembering your roots and what it took to get you where you are now. Write a note or place a call to someone who helped you along the way and thank him or her for what they did for you. Pay special attention to how taking these actions makes you feel.

Sophia Cho Johnson

23

The World Class Never Bows To Criticism

"You can't let praise or criticism get to you. It's a weakness to get caught up in either one."

– John Wooden, Hall of Fame basketball coach, University of California Los Angeles

Mental toughness, broken down to its root, is really about becoming a master of your emotions in performance situations, especially under pressure. The fastest way to differentiate an amateur from a pro is to observe how they respond to criticism. Amateurs are shocked when they are criticized, and many are emotionally wounded. Professional performers expect criticism as a part of being a champion and are rarely rattled by it. The mentally tough expect little from their amateur-thinking counterparts, and when they are criticized, they often sum it up as amateurs mud slinging. Professional performers rarely criticize other people – they're too busy working and practicing to get wrapped up in other people's business. They don't deal in personalities; they deal in ideas. Professional performers aren't surprised by criticism from average people. They realize they are a mirror into which amateurs look, only to see themselves for what they really are – average. World-class performers make them look lazy and unmotivated by comparison, and they resent it, so they lash out and criticize. Meanwhile, champions ignore the criticism and go back to work.

▶ **ACTION STEP FOR TODAY**

Decide to separate your emotions from other people's criticism of you. Refuse to talk about other people or gossip about their behavior. Focus only on ideas that can help you fulfill your vision.

24

Champions Believe In Choice

"Everything can be taken from a man but one thing: the last of the human freedoms – to choose one's attitude in any given set of circumstances, to choose one's own way."
– Viktor Frankel, 1905-1997, psychiatrist, author, and lecturer

Just as amateurs see themselves as victims of circumstance, professional performers believe they possess the ultimate human freedom – the power to choose. Average people get out of bed in the morning and say, "I have to go to work." Champions know they don't have to do anything they choose not to do. This mindset impacts every decision of both amateurs and professionals. Amateurs feel they are at the mercy of the gods; professionals carefully construct a life based on a series of choices they make. This sense of control increases the professionals' ambitious drive. It's also one of the reasons champions appear to be so much happier than average people. They know their choices really control their destiny. They believe they can be anyone they want to be, do anything they want to do, and have anything they want to have. Their belief in this concept becomes a self-fulfilling prophecy, which builds psychological momentum and makes the belief stronger every day.

► ACTION STEP FOR TODAY

Make a list of the things you feel you have no choice about doing, and revisit each one. Do you really have to do them, or are you choosing to do them? Could some of the less desirable things be omitted simply by making a choice? Delusion says you

I am choosing to do them

must do these things. Objective reality says you always have a choice, because you are always in control.

▶▶I **WORLD-CLASS RESOURCE**
Read Choice Theory, by Dr. William Glasser. This is a great book that removes any sense of victim mentality any of us may have.

25

The World Class Embraces Metacognition

"Of course we become what we think about. The real question is, "Do we know what we are thinking about?"
— *Steve Siebold*

When it comes to thoughts, feelings and attitudes, the masses are heavily influenced by external forces, like a pinball being bounced around from bumper to bumper. Their outer world determines their inner world. World-class thinkers are just the opposite. Knowing their thoughts control their feelings, the great ones have adopted the habit of thinking about . . . what they think about. Psychologists refer to this as "Metacognition." This championship habit enables the performer to get to the root of the thoughts that bring about both positive and negative feelings. Once the performer is aware of the thoughts that are ultimately creating his results, he has the power to change any thought he chooses. In essence, metacognition enables the performer to take control of his thought processes. This makes the champions' reality directly opposite of the masses, in that the great ones' inner world determines their outer world. In other words, the results they achieve on the outside are dictated by the thoughts they have on the inside. The masses are victims of their own thoughts. They have the same potential for greatness as the pros do, yet are simply not paying attention to what they are allowing to enter their minds, and the results are disastrous. Meanwhile, the world class is thriving on upgraded thoughts that are manifesting tremendous results. They know that the better they become at controlling their thoughts, the better their results will be, and it all begins with metacognition.

▶ ACTION STEP FOR TODAY

Take your emotional temperature today and assess your mood. Ask this critical thinking question: "How did I end up in this mood?" What thoughts did you process that put you in this mood?

26

Professional Performers Don't Require Immediate Compensation

"Did you think you could have the good without the evil?
Did you think you could have the joy without the sorrow?"
– David Grayson, professor and author

Most people are fully engaged in microwave thinking – a deep belief that compensation should immediately follow any effort. Champions are different. They believe every effort performed with good intention yields some form of compensation at some point. People become champions by perfecting their competencies until other people label them 'champion.' In most cases, this label took years of hard work and sacrifice to achieve, with little or no apparent compensation along the way. Many of the great ones were ridiculed and criticized for investing so many hours in the development of their core competency. Not swayed by amateur opinion, they pushed forward aggressively. This delayed gratification set the stage for all future battle plans for achievement in the minds of champions. When professional performers set a big goal, they are expecting a fight – and their past experience has preconditioned their minds for battle. When amateurs expect compensation, pros are just settling in for the fight. Their willingness to delay gratification and compensation makes them more valuable in the marketplace.

▶ **ACTION STEP FOR TODAY**

Ask this critical thinking question: "Am I more interested in pleasure, or gratification?" Amateurs focus on pleasure-based activities that deliver short and sweet payoffs. Professionals focus on gratification-based activities that take longer to achieve but deliver long and deep payoffs. Into which category do you fall?

27
Champions Embrace Conflict For Growth

"A good manager doesn't try to eliminate conflict, he
tries to keep it from wasting the energies of his people.
If you're the boss and your people fight you openly
when they think you're wrong – that's healthy."

– Robert Townsend, former CEO, Avis Rent-a-Car

Average performers will do almost anything to avoid conflict. World-class performers not only welcome it, but embrace it. Amateurs derive their approach from an emotional perspective, while professionals ground their approach in logic. An emotional response comes from the fear of suffering a bruised ego, because average people would rather be accepted by others than realize a superior solution to a problem. Conflict represents a serious emotional threat to fragile constitutions. The great ones see conflict not as a threat, but as an opportunity to gain a three-dimensional perspective on a problem. The pros operate at a higher level of consciousness and don't care who gets the credit for solving the problem. Logic dictates their actions and opens their minds to the possibility that the opposition may be right. Champions see conflict as a healthy function of checks and balances in an organization. Dictatorships and organizations which suppress conflict are too tightly bound to allow opportunities for growth. Organizations which welcome or embrace conflict are destined to evolve exponentially from the combined brainpower of the group.

not who's right but what is right

▶ **ACTION STEP FOR TODAY**

Ask this critical thinking question: "Am I emotionally addicted to the approval of others?" If your answer is yes, make a commitment to break this addiction immediately.

28

Champions Are Comeback Artists

> "I'm going to the top of the mountain. You're either going to see me waving from the top or dead on the side. But you know what? I'm not coming down."
>
> — *Eric Worre, author, speaker*

When Donald Trump was $9 billion dollars in debt in the early 1990s, did you really believe he was washed up for good? After Lance Armstrong survived cancer, did anyone really think he wouldn't race again? How about Christopher Reeve? Did anyone really bet against him making an international impact to help people with spinal cord injuries, once he made the decision to do it? There's an old saying among the world class: "A bet against a champion is a bad bet." I couldn't agree more. Amateurs quickly become demoralized by setbacks and defeat, and quietly slink back to their comfort zones. Professional performers know that large-scale success is based on a series of comebacks. They believe that setbacks are set-ups for comebacks. Amateurs often make the mistake of counting professionals out when things get tough. The average person grossly underestimates the level of mental toughness that champions possess. The great ones will comeback out of nowhere, just when everyone has counted them out. Emotionally speaking, they don't really understand the concept of giving up. I don't mean this as an insult. They understand how to quit intellectually. But emotionally, they have been hard wired through years of world-class programming to focus on a vision and persevere at any cost. This is why rock-solid character is critical to this group. The only thing that can stop this speeding locomotive from its destination is the potential harm or destruction of others. The great ones never sacrifice people for success. The upper class is so ego-driven they often run over anyone who gets in their way. The world class, guided by their spirit-based consciousness, will only proceed toward their visions if their actions are fair to all parties concerned. Once this has been established, the champions fail again and again; yet continue coming back for more. On the physical plane, we call it perseverance. On the mental plane, we call it toughness. On the spiritual plane, we call it artistry.

▶ ACTION STEP FOR TODAY

Identify a goal or dream in your life that you have given up on, and ask this critical thinking question: "Is it possible to make a comeback in this area, and breathe new life into this old dream?" You're a tougher, more competent performer than you were back when you abandoned this dream. Are you good enough to make a comeback now? (Hint: YES!)

29

The Great Ones Are Masters Of Their Work/Rest Cycles

"Recovery is an important word and a vital concept. It means renewal of life and energy. Knowing how and when to recover may prove to be the most important skill in your life."

— James E. Loehr, Ed.D, author, psychologist

Average people refuse to recognize one of the most critical aspects of peak performance: cycles. If human beings were robots, performance experts like myself wouldn't consult with our clients about the proper use of cycles. Yet we're not robots. We are, primarily, emotionally driven creatures whose level of performance is dictated by what we believe and how we feel at any given time. Most amateur performers never push themselves hard enough to ever warrant any concern with cycles, but for champions, it can make the difference between winning and losing. The great ones know (or are trained to know) when to exert maximum effort and when to let their mind and body rest. The enemy of all champions is physical and emotional burnout, and they will go to great lengths in the performance planning process to insure burnout never occurs more than once. Most world-class coaches will push their performers to the breaking point at least one time to establish how far that individual can be pushed. Every performer has a different tolerance for pain. When this breaking point is established, a cycle of stress and recovery is implemented. Time off and life balance are key factors in performance cycles – as are massive influxes of effort. The great ones know the magic is in the mix.

▶ **ACTION STEP FOR TODAY**

Give yourself a life balance checkup. Are you investing the necessary time and energy in the important areas of your life? What areas are you over-stressing? What areas are you under-stressing? Think about your current stress and recovery cycles and make any adjustments you think are necessary for peak performance and maximum happiness.

▶▶❘ **WORLD-CLASS RESOURCE**

Read Stress for Success, by Dr. James Loehr.

30

The World Class Is Coachable

*"Great coaching is helping people discover
what they already know."*

– Bill Gove, 1912-2001, the father of professional speaking

Corporate America and entrepreneurs are starting to catch on to something athletes have always known: if you want to maximize your potential in anything, hire a coach. Coaching is to performance what leadership is to an organization. Since human beings are primarily emotional creatures, competent coaches are experts at stoking the fires that burn within – assuming there is already (at least) a small flame. Coaches can't create the flame, but the good ones can turn a small flame into a blow torch. World-class coaches won't even accept a client if they fail to find a flame inside. They know the flame is the prerequisite for greatness. Average people will only accept the amount of coaching their egos will allow. Champions are well known for being the most open to world-class coaching. The bigger the champion, the more open-minded they are. The great ones couldn't care less about ego satisfaction when it comes to improving their results – all they're looking for is an edge, no matter how slight. Their logic behind this is simple: when two champions go head to head, many times the only thing that favors the winner is a slight edge in thinking, strategy and technique. All champions look for that one little advantage that great coaching can provide.

▶ **ACTION STEP FOR TODAY**

Invest 15 minutes to consider hiring a coach to help you get better results. Be coachable and open-minded. You may be surprised at what you will learn.

▶▶I **WORLD-CLASS RESOURCE**

For private, semiprivate and small group coaching, visit www.mentaltoughnesscollege.com

---

31

Champions Are Mentally Engaged In The Creative Process

"The creative person wants to know about all kinds of things: ancient history, nineteenth-century mathematics, current manufacturing techniques, flower arranging, and hog futures, because he never knows when these ideas might come together to form a new idea."

– Carl Ally, founder, Ally & Gargano Advertising

While average people are satisfied with the status quo, world-class performers are always searching for new ideas and new ways to interpret old ideas. They do this by tapping into to the right hemisphere of their brain, the more creative side. Champions believe there is always a better, easier, faster way to accomplish anything and being creative is the way to discover it. One of the methods they use to stoke their creative flow is to learn, study and be interested in a variety of different things. The discovery of a truth in an unrelated subject could easily be transferred to a current problem. There is a level of relativity and relationship to the order of all things, and the great ones know it. Champions discover these truths because they pay attention – not because they're smarter than anyone else. The masses are not mentally engaged. Their billion-dollar thought processing system is used for activities like watching television and figuring out how to travel the road of least resistance. Meanwhile, champions are being mentally reborn daily as a result of making new distinctions, interpretations and discoveries . . . and then they use these ideas to solve their problems.

▶ ACTION STEP FOR TODAY

Rate yourself on a scale of 1 to 7, 7 being most creative. Be honest. How creative are you?

▶▶I WORLD-CLASS RESOURCE

The best book I've read on creativity is The Artist's Way, by Julia Cameron. This book will help unlock the genius inside you. The best speaker I've heard on the subject of creativity is Gregg Fraley, of Chicago. You can learn more about Gregg at www.greggfraley.com

32

Champions Operate With A Clear Conscience

"Reason often makes mistakes, but conscience never does."
— Josh Billings, 1818-1885, writer

The world class tends to rely on intuition and conscience much more often than the masses. While average people are more concerned with what other people think of their actions, professional performers answer to a jury of one: their conscience. One reason they're able to maintain such high levels of concentration and intensity in their field of expertise is because they rarely carry mental baggage. With their conscience as their guide, champions often have greater mental clarity and internal focus than average people. Rotary International, (www.rotary.org), an organization of business champions performing community service on a global level, has a great tool called the four-way test. The idea is for Rotarians to answer four questions before making any major decision.

The questions are:

1) Is it the truth?
2) Is it fair to all concerned?
3) Will it build goodwill and better friendships?
4) Will it be beneficial to all concerned?

The world class often follows such formulas in making important decisions. Champions know they can often fool other people, but they can never fool themselves. Amateurs pay a serious price for making decisions that are incongruent with their conscience, and their self-image is the first thing that suffers. The

great ones know this is too high a price to pay. Self-image expert
Nathaniel Branden says, "Self-esteem is the reputation we acquire
with ourselves." Being in touch and living by their conscience is a
hallmark of mentally tough performers.

▶ **ACTION STEP FOR TODAY**

Ask this critical thinking question: "Are all of my dealings congruent with my conscience?" If the answer is yes, you empower
yourself to success. If not, consider abandoning these deals or
behaviors. Universal law dictates that whatever you sow, you
shall reap.

33

Common Sense Is The Foundation Of High Performance

*"Common sense is the knack of seeing things as they
are, and doing things as they ought to be done."*
– *Harriet Beecher Stowe, 1811-1896, author of Uncle Tom's Cabin*

Champions usually believe the essentials of life were learned in
kindergarten. Their world view is that success is simple and
constructed fundamentally from common sense. While average
people search for complex answers to their problems, the world
class looks for the simple solution first – and usually finds it. They
solve more complex challenges by looking at the situation as an
outsider viewing it for the first time. Larry Wilson, the famous
speaker and author, says the great ones get out of their own way
by viewing the problem from ten thousand feet in order to gain
a new perspective. They separate themselves from the everyday
details and gain a three-dimensional view of the problem. While
average people strain to create a solution, champions think for a

while and then create a mental distance to take their direct focus off the problem. Many times the answers come to them in the shower, in the middle of the night, or at the health club while they're working out. The law of indirect effort is one of the most powerful problem-solving processes known to man. Champions realize the secret to tapping their true genius is sometimes hidden in the act of not trying so hard.

[handwritten margin note: Let asm work for you. The answer will come.]

▶ ACTION STEP FOR TODAY

Write down your five most pressing problems and ask: "Is there a kindergarten answer to this seemingly complex problem?" Let your mind revert to childlike thinking and write down the first answers that come to mind.

34

Champions Always Strive For Greater Competence

"Information is the booby prize. The real prize is competence."
– Larry Wilson, founder, Wilson Learning Corp.

Amateur performers are often good at memorizing and learning bits and pieces of information, just as they were taught to do in school. Champions know memorizing data in the information age is worth about as much as it costs to purchase a computer and log on to the Internet. Champions are focused on becoming competent at what they do, and leave the information gathering to someone else. While the masses worry about job security and the return of poor economic conditions, champions spend time building and improving their attitude, skills and knowledge in their chosen field. This laser-guided focus channels energy directly to the building blocks of their competency. This approach puts professional performers in constant demand from corporations and organizations searching for people with world-class habits. So, while amateurs stay up at night worrying about job security, the pros are quietly creating it through competence. The future belongs to the competent, both in their field and in terms of controlling and directing their emotions. But then again, it always has.

▶ ACTION STEP FOR TODAY

List the three most important activities in which you must continue to develop competence. Make a commitment to invest a set number of hours per week (beyond your normal working hours) to study. One hour of extra study per day in your chosen field will make you a national expert in five years or less.

▶▶▎ WORLD-CLASS RESOURCE

The ultimate common sense guide to success is Think and Grow Rich, by Napoleon Hill. This classic was written in 1937 and has since become the book by which all personal development books are measured. It's a must-read for anyone interested in world-class results.

35

Champions Develop Bravery In The Battle For Their Dream

"The world has a way of giving what is demanded of it. If you are frightened and look for failure and poverty, you will get them, no matter how hard you may try to succeed. Lack of faith in yourself, in what life will do for you, cuts you off from the good things of the world. Expect victory and you make victory. Nowhere is this truer than in business life, where bravery and faith bring both material and spiritual rewards."

– Preston Bradley

World-class performers know facing their biggest doubts, fears and worries are the ultimate challenges for champions, and therefore exercise a substantial amount of bravery in their lives. They are willing to endure sleepless nights and endless worries as they walk the razor's edge. They're profoundly aware that one small slip could send everything they've built crashing down, yet they continue to build. They are often criticized and ridiculed by the masses, who see them as a threat to their lack of engagement in life. Champions accept the fact that the end result to life is the same for everyone, and since no one will survive in the end, there is no point in playing it safe. So, what average people see as unnecessary risk taking, champions view as playing the game while there's still time left on the clock. They have the guts and bravery to face the truth and take risks that make the masses squirm.

▶ **ACTION STEP FOR TODAY**

Make a list of ten things you're afraid to do, and decide to push past your fear and do one of them. The sense of exhilaration you'll feel will only be exceeded by the confidence you'll gain.

▶▶◀ **WORLD-CLASS RESOURCE**

Invest ten minutes in reading a few of the stories and prayers written by parents who have a child fighting cancer. These people are some of the bravest on the planet. Visit www. kidscancernetwork.org/prayerlist.html

36

Champions Hold Strong Convictions

"What convinces is conviction. You must believe in the argument you are advancing."
— *Lyndon Johnson, 1908-1973, U.S. President*

One hallmark of world-class performers is their level of conviction in who they are and what they do. Champion's beliefs and convictions are so strong that it's contagious. Professional performers who passionately believe in their convictions have the power to influence people and change the world. The great ones are easy to recognize — you can see it in their eyes and hear it in their voices. The famous minister John Wesley is a great example. Historians say; "Rev. Wesley's conviction and passion was so strong, that when he spoke it was as if his soul was on fire, and people would travel from miles around just to watch him burn." My research and experience shows that champions are not more passionate about everything. Champions go to extraordinary lengths to discover the work in which their deepest passions lie, and then turn their flame of desire into a blow torch of healthy obsession. Average people usually don't invest the time necessary to discover where their passions lie. Instead, amateurs tend to implement distractions that are entertaining (at best), or a way to shield themselves from failure (at worst). These distractions include television, spectator sports, hobbies, booze, and drugs. It's far easier to boo and cheer a million-dollar athlete than it is to become one. Generally speaking, amateurs are spectators in the game of life. And it all begins with their lack of desire to discover their convictions.

▶ ACTION STEP FOR TODAY

On a scale of 1 to 7, 7 being the most, how much conviction do you possess about the importance of your work? If you answered less than 7, what can you do to boost your level of conviction?

37

The Great Ones Know The Power Of Conversation

"A conversation is a dialogue, not a monologue.
That's why there are so few good conversations: due
to scarcity, two intelligent talkers seldom meet."
– Truman Capote, 1924-1984, novelist

One of the primary differences between the masses and world-class performers is how much attention they pay to developing their conversational skills. Champions master the art of interpersonal communication. They know their success is directly proportional to the number of advocates they have in their professional network of contacts. The great ones treat their databases like sacred artifacts, because they know those lists of people are priceless. They build their network one-by-one, and stay in constant, but unobtrusive, contact with the fervor of a presidential candidate rallying support. Champions know that, if they lost everything they owned, they could pick up a phone, contact their network, and be back in business in nothing flat. The great ones are in awe of the massive power of their network. Networks usually begin and develop through a series of conversations. World-class performers are charismatic conversationalists. They achieve this by focusing their conversation on the other people, getting them to talk about their lives. Professional performers are usually the people asking the questions and paying rapt attention to the answers. Champions focus their part of the conversation on ideas, concepts, and things of a positive nature. They refuse to discuss other people in a way that discredits them or adversely affects their reputation.

▶ **ACTION STEP FOR TODAY**

Commit to becoming a student of interpersonal communication. This single skill will do more to help you move toward world-class results than any other.

▶▶▎ **WORLD-CLASS RESOURCE**

Read How to Win Friends and Influence People, by Dale Carnegie. This is arguably the greatest book ever written on interpersonal communication skills.

38

Champions Are Decisive

"If I had to sum up in one word what makes a good manager, I'd say decisiveness. You can use the fanciest computers to gather the numbers, but in the end you have to set a timetable and act."

– Lee Iacocca, former chairman, Chrysler Corp.

While average performers are timid and lack confidence in their own judgment, champions are known for their ability to make decisions, especially under pressure. The difference is courage and confidence. Even the best leaders are uncertain about their decisions in an environment of unprecedented change. The difference is their willingness to make a decision and take full responsibility for the outcome. Amateur performers habitually play not to lose and procrastinate because they fear making a mistake. The great ones know mistakes will be made and can be corrected. Their willingness to assume full responsibility for their decisions eliminates the need to gather more input than is absolutely necessary. Developing a sound decision-making process, while understanding every decision is somewhat a gamble, is the foundation of superior leadership. Professional performers can lead people and organizations effectively under such high-pressure constraints because they possess the self-trust necessary to make decisions without fear. Generally speaking, the higher the leadership position, the greater and the deeper the leader's self-trust must be. Courage, self-trust and the willingness to assume full responsibility for the outcomes of their decisions are mandatory traits of competent and effective leaders.

▶ ACTION STEP FOR TODAY

Take a decision you have been putting off for a while and decide on a course of action within the next 24 hours. Decision-making skills are like muscles: they can only be built through use.

▶▶▌ WORLD-CLASS RESOURCE

Read Grow Up! by Dr. Frank Pittman. This book takes a no-holds-barred approach to taking personal responsibility.

39

The Great Ones Choose
Discipline Over Pleasure

"With self-discipline anything is possible. I believe
discipline is the ultimate key to success as it determines
your approach toward every day. Discipline keeps you
focused and keeps you performing at a world-class level."
– Roger D. Graham Jr.

When average performers have had enough for the day and call it quits, champions are usually just getting started. Discipline is the watchword of great performers. Discipline makes the difference between the good and the great. The great ones will tell you discipline is more of a decision than it is an active skill. It's the ability to stay the course and complete promises you've made. The fulfillment of these promises builds confidence and self-esteem, which eventually leads the champions to believe almost anything is possible. It's a habit and a self-fulfilling prophecy built into one. Discipline is a logic-based decision that performers adhere to, regardless of whether they feel like it or not. Discipline pushes performers past pain and punishment. As my late business partner and mentor Bill Gove always said, "It's easier to act yourself into good thinking than it is to think yourself into good action." This is the mindset of the champion. The great ones, like Bill Gove, don't let feelings interfere with their performance. Instead, they harness the power of their emotional motivators to propel them past the competition. Average people see discipline as a painful chore to be avoided at all costs. The world class sees it as the ultimate power tool for performance.

▶ **ACTION STEP FOR TODAY**

On a scale of 1 to 7, 7 being most disciplined, how disciplined are you in the different areas of your life? Categories include business/career; family/friends; money/finances; recreation/fun; health/diet/exercise; faith/spiritual; social/cultural; and personal development.

40

The World Class Is Determined To Win

"**Winning isn't everything, but wanting to win is.**"
– *Vince Lombardi, 1913-1970, legendary coach, Green Bay Packers*

As simple as it sounds, many times the only thing that separates winners from losers is pure determination. While the winning difference may be slight, the thought process that makes the difference is huge. Amateur performers spend a substantial amount of time negotiating the price of victory. Amateurs seem to have an endless tape looping through their minds, asking, "Is the effort worth the reward for winning?" Meanwhile, champions focus on winning. Their attitude is, "Whatever it takes." Champions don't negotiate their efforts and sacrifices enroute to victory. The decision to pay any price and bear any burden in the name of victory was made long before the game started. This subtle difference in thinking is a huge advantage. Nowhere is this more apparent than when pain occurs. Amateurs feel pain and seek escape. Professionals expect to feel pain and have been mentally trained to push past it while maintaining a world-class level of performance. Champions are the warriors of the world. Their outstanding preparation, both mental and physical, makes them unstoppable and ferocious on any performance field.

▶ ACTION STEP FOR TODAY

On a scale of 1 to 7, 7 being most determined, how determined are you to accomplish your goals and dreams? An assessment of the results you have achieved so far is an accurate measure of how determined you have been in the past.

▶▶◀ WORLD-CLASS RESOURCE

Even though it was fiction, Rocky has to be the all-time classic portrayal of world-class determination. The world is full of Rocky-like stories of people who refused to take no for an answer when manifesting their vision. If you haven't seen Rocky, rent it; if you have seen it, rent it again. As you're watching the movie, ask this critical thinking question: "Do I have this level of determination with my vision?" If you have a big vision, Rocky-like determination is probably what it's going to take to make it reality.

41

Champions Dedicate Their Lives To Greatness

"To succeed in life, one must have determination and must be prepared to suffer during the process. If one isn't prepared to suffer during adversities, I don't really see how he can be successful."

– Gary Player, professional golfer

Professional performers are the most dedicated people alive. While amateurs are dedicated when things are going well, champions are always dedicated. In other words, it's not what they do, it's who they are. The great ones don't know any other way. Their dedication to excellence shines through in everything they do. Dedication is a habit they've developed; it serves as a cornerstone of their success and fulfillment in life. Average people are more dedicated to pleasure than performance. The top 1% of world-class performers invest thousands of dollars every year on self-development books, DVDs, CDs, seminars, workshops and retreats. Most amateur performers haven't read a book since high school and wouldn't attend a self-development seminar unless you paid them. The masses tend to believe education ends with high school or college graduation. The world class tends to believe formal education only teaches you how to learn, cope and manage yourself in the world as an adult. They believe real education begins after school lets out. Dedication to getting what they want from life is a driving force behind champions. While the masses seek perpetual pleasure, the great ones focus on achievement. The irony is that professional performers tend to experience great pleasure as a result of their achievements. Such feelings of accomplishment and fulfillment are an additional benefit only the great ones enjoy.

▶ ACTION STEP FOR TODAY

Ask this critical thinking question: "How much am I willing to struggle and suffer to make my vision a reality?" Is it a little, a fair amount, a lot, or whatever it takes?

▶▶ WORLD-CLASS RESOURCE

Pick a biography of your favorite champion and read it cover to cover. This will give you an idea of the level of dedication it takes to become one of the great ones. Next month, read another biography. After a few of these books, you'll begin to see a pattern in each champion's thinking and dedication to their dream. Develop the habit of reading biographies of world-class performers and you'll reap the benefits of their wisdom and experience.

42

Champions Are Driven
By A World-Class Belief System

"In the second grade, they asked us what we wanted to be. I said
I wanted to be a ball player, and they laughed. In eighth grade,
they asked the same question, and I said a ball player, and they
laughed a little more. By the eleventh grade, no one was laughing."

– Johnny Bench, major league catcher

Make no mistake: champions are driven to succeed. Many
believe that only some people are born with this innate
aptitude of ambition. Studies show this isn't true. Champions are
driven to win, in most cases, because they believe they can. If you
inherited a treasure map from your best friend, would you be driven
to follow the map and find the fortune? So would anyone else. If
this is true, why are the majority of people simply trying to survive
in a world of wealth and abundance? The answer is simple: they
don't believe they can find their own treasure. This doesn't alter
the fact that the treasure is there, yet it does change the drive of
the performer. The human animal is only driven to the level their
belief system will allow. Most of us have been programmed by
amateur performers with limited belief systems, and subsequently,
small ambitions. As a result, they tend to attract other amateurs as
friends, who reinforce these limited beliefs and validate their lack
consciousness. This cycle spins out of control until the drive is
nearly nonexistent. Amateurs rationalize their lack of drive with
tall tales of bad breaks and unfortunate circumstances. Meanwhile,
the champions – no more intelligent or talented – become more
focused and driven every day and continue to win.

▶ ACTION STEP FOR TODAY

Generally speaking, is your belief system poverty class, middle class, or world class? Ask this critical thinking question: "Do my drive and ambition mirror my beliefs?" If you're not sure of the answer, check your results in the areas of your life where you exhibit the most ambition.

43

The World Class Has Great Expectations

"As your consciousness expands, your level of
expectation will grow. Keep asking yourself, am
I selling myself short? Most of us are."

– John R. Spannuth, President, United
States Water Fitness Association

One of the greatest discoveries I've made in the last two decades as a mental toughness coach is the realization that world-class performers are driven by positive expectations. In other words, the great ones always expect to win regardless of what they are up against. The next discovery I made was that this same positive expectation could be installed in anyone who wishes to possess it. It's a programming process that is easy to do; all it takes is desire and persistence. Champions begin this programming process by creating the language they use when they talk to themselves, as well as the pictures they visualize. World-class performers literally talk themselves into believing anything that gives them a mental edge. Call it positive brainwashing, programming, affirmation training, auto-suggestion – whatever label you choose. Champions call it their ace in the hole. While most amateur performers rely on positive experience to build positive expectation, professional performers are superstars in their minds long before they are superstars in reality. Why wait for Mother Nature to produce snow at a ski resort when it can be artificially produced right now? Then, when it does snow, it simply adds powder to a very solid base. Expectation works whether it's built from real experience or programming. The advantage of programming is it is guaranteed to happen – while experience may or may not occur.

▶ ACTION STEP FOR TODAY

Outline your expectations in every area of your life, and then ask the ultimate critical thinking question: "Should I expect more?" If your answer is yes, raise your expectations and upgrade how you talk to yourself and others about your heightened aspirations.

▶▶│ WORLD-CLASS RESOURCE

Build a personal and professional board of advisors, comprised of people who have a much higher level of expectation than you. Spend as much time with them as possible. One of the fastest ways to raise your level of expectation is to associate with world-class thinkers. To see my National Board of Advisors, go to www.govesiebold.com There's an in-depth interview with each member of our board, which will give you a better feel for who these people are and how they think.

44

The Great Ones Are The Most Enthusiastic People Alive

"All we really need to make us happy is
something to be enthusiastic about."
— *Charles Kingsley, 1819-1875, novelist*

All professional performers have discovered the real secret of greatness: enthusiasm for what they do. Champions are driven by an enthusiasm that fires their soul and keeps them on the practice field long after everyone else has gone home. The great ones know the raw, unbridled power of an enthusiastic mindset. Amateurs tend to be more enthusiastic about the accomplishments of others, such as actors, sports stars and musicians. While amateurs are spending their enthusiasm on batting averages and the box office, professional performers are investing their life energy into their field of choice. Champions are willing to put themselves on the line and risk failure and rejection, while amateurs sit on the sidelines and observe without risk. Champions often have the world view that life is a game to play to the best of their ability, with enthusiasm and tenacity, until their hearts stop beating. Amateurs often think life is something to struggle through while avoiding pain at all costs. My friend and mentor, Larry Wilson, has a great vision of their arrival at the pearly gates: The amateur arrives, and Saint Peter says, "Congratulations. You've arrived safely at death." Champions know having something to be enthusiastic about is one the most important ingredients of a happy life. The great ones are either engaged in or actively seeking their passion everyday.

▶ **ACTION STEP FOR TODAY**

Make a list of the five activities in your life for which you have the most enthusiasm. Next, ask this critical thinking question: "Does anyone make a living doing this?"

▶▶▌ **WORLD-CLASS RESOURCE**

Read Do What You Love and the Money Will Follow, by Marsha Sinetar. If you are in the process of trying to figure out what you really want to do with your career, this book may have the answer.

45

Champions Love What They Do

"I'd rather be a failure at something I love than a success at something I don't."
– *George Burns, 1896-1996, comedian*

It doesn't seem to matter what industry, profession, occupation or sport champions choose – the criteria for selection is almost always enjoyment. Champions tend to choose their field based on pure enjoyment of the activity. Some people say that champions don't pick their field, the field picks them. Amateurs believe champions enjoy their work because they are successful. Yet interviews with the superstars find the polar opposite to be true. Champions are successful because they enjoy their work. As a result, they put their heart and soul into the activity, so much so that they surpass their competitors. College students of yesterday were often told to study business or computers, or law or medicine, because of the great financial potential. This single idea has probably created more average performers than any other. The progressive mindset of the 21st century is to study what you enjoy studying and put your heart and soul into it. The great ones know that money doesn't come from an occupation; it comes from solving people's problems. Champions do so much extra study and work that they become experts, and often become wealthy as a result. Professional performers not only see enjoying what they do as a philosophy, they see it as their single greatest asset and entry into the world class.

▶ ACTION STEP FOR TODAY

On a scale of 1 to 7, 7 being the most enjoyment, how much do you enjoy your job? If you answered less than a 7, the odds of fulfilling your full potential are slim. If you answered a 7, then you will almost assuredly ascend to the world-class level.

▶▶◄ WORLD-CLASS RESOURCE

Read Work Happy Live Healthy, by Tom Welch. Visit www. workhappy.com

---

46

Champions Create A Winning Environment

"The first step toward success is taken when you refuse to be a captive of the environment in which you first find yourself."
– Mark Caine, author

Have you ever noticed children of super-rich families often attract misery into their lives in a variety of ways? These children are raised in an environment of extreme privilege. As a result, they often develop a sense of entitlement that creates conflicting feelings as their lives progress. Even at age forty, some of these 'kids' are completely confused about how they fit into the world, because they never had an opportunity to learn and grow through adversity and challenge. Their parents purchased their problems away, and left them with a gaping psychological hole. Similarly, amateur performers tend to be their own worst enemies, and create misery and depression from a deep sense of disappointment with themselves. Professional performers learn to create their own environment of ongoing learning, growth and discipline. They often discover their greatest joy in the conquering of their greatest obstacles. While amateurs do everything possible to exist in an environment of comfort, champions know the only true comfort comes from becoming the people they were meant to be by learning and growing each day. Amateurs think they are victims of their environment, and seem to thrive on blaming other people. Professional performers realize the people who programmed them did the best they could, based on their level of awareness, and then take the necessary steps to reprogram themselves and create the world-class environment they deserve.

▶ ACTION STEP FOR TODAY

Make a commitment to upgrade your environment, beginning with the people around you. Limit your exposure to neutral and negative people, remembering that consciousness is contagious. Befriend a champion and spend as much time with this person as possible. I promise this will raise your level of expectation.

▶▶I WORLD-CLASS RESOURCE

Become an active student of personal development by listening to tapes and CDs from your favorite authors, speakers and philosophers as you drive. Create a world-class environment by turning your car into a university on wheels. The largest producer of personal development tapes and CDs is Nightingale-Conant Corp.; their website is www.nightingale. com

47

The World Class Makes Exercise A Priority

"Exercise is king. Nutrition is queen. Put the two of them together and you have a kingdom."

— Jack Lalane, fitness guru

Amateurs tend to believe exercise is only for the young, and that it has little to do with success in the business world. Studies show this to be false. In the last ten years, many companies have started corporate exercise programs and constructed workout facilities on company premises. They know regular exercise is the single most significant aspect of good health, and good employee health goes right to the bottom line. Champions have known this for years. They tend to invest at least an hour per day, every day, in some form of physical activity. They usually select an activity they really enjoy to insure it will become a habit. Amateurs spend more time watching their favorite sports heroes exercise than they do exercising themselves. The cost of this inactive lifestyle is substantial, both physically and mentally. Professional performers know a sound mind and sound body are one and the same, and they treat their physical activity with the same intensity and priority as they do their work. They schedule daily exercise and approach it with the same vigor as a meeting with a key customer. The biggest distinction between amateurs and pros in this area is the importance they place on adhering to their exercise routine. Amateurs see exercise as a chore; pros see it as a necessity for world-class performance.

▶ **ACTION STEP FOR TODAY**

Make a commitment to exercise for at least one hour per day, five days a week. The excuse that you don't have time is a delusion. Exercise is necessary for a long and healthy life. Get your calendar out and move things around to make room for exercise, no matter what it takes. Your life literally depends on it.

▶▶▎ **WORLD-CLASS RESOURCE**

If you're a man, subscribe to Men's Health magazine. If you're a woman, subscribe to Shape Magazine. Visit www.menshealth.com or www.shape.com

48

The Great Ones Are Professional Failures

"There can be no failure to a man who has not lost his courage, his character, his self-respect, or his self-confidence. He is still a king."
— *Orison Swett Marden, 1848-1924, founder, Success Magazine*

The majority of the differences between amateurs and pros is a subtle separation. It's a slight difference in thinking that makes a big difference in results. The idea of failure is an example of this. Amateurs tend to believe failure is painful and should be avoided in order to maintain a sense of pride and dignity. In an effort to protect their egos, they attempt only those things they know they can do. Champions see failure as a necessary building block of mega-success, and treat it as a teacher. People labeled as failures are amateurs at failing. Successful people are professional failures, who have failed their way to success. The difference is their mental approach. Champions aren't in the business of protecting their egos; they're in the business of learning, growing and becoming. They see failures as necessary course adjustments – not always pleasant, yet necessary to gain the wisdom and mental toughness it's going to take to make their vision a reality. While amateurs spend a lot of time focusing on how not to fail, pros are dialed in to doing what it takes to succeed. This problem-solving, execution-based focus creates a greater awareness of more potential solutions. A focus on failure prevention creates an awareness of fear, lack and poverty. It's all a matter of where a performer places his attention.

▶ ACTION STEP FOR TODAY

Ask this critical thinking question: "Have I been playing it safe to avoid failure?" On a scale of 1 to 7, 7 being the highest, how many risks have you taken in an effort to make your vision a reality?

▶▶ WORLD-CLASS RESOURCE

If you're in the world of selling, read How I Raised Myself from Failure to Success in Selling, by Frank Bettger. This book is a detailed account of how one man figured out how the system works. The great Dale Carnegie called this book, "The most helpful and inspiring book on salesmanship I have ever read." It's a must for your sales library.

49

Champions Have Tremendous Faith

"We do not need more intellectual power; we need more
spiritual power . . . . We do not need more of the things that
are seen, we need more of the things that are unseen."
– *Calvin Coolidge, 1872-1933, U.S. President*

Faith has always been a hallmark of world-class performers –
most notably, the faith performers have in themselves. The
great ones have an extremely high level of self-trust, even when
they are failing. This faith in self may stem from being raised in a
positive environment, or from performers talking themselves into
it. Muhammad Ali admits he told the world he was the greatest
before he truly was as a way to bolster his faith in his own skills.
(I think it worked!) Champions also have faith in their goals and
dreams becoming reality, while amateurs are often deathly afraid
of believing in something that may or may not happen. Faith in
God, a higher power, or an infinite intelligence is also a trait of
many champions. There are atheists who are tremendous performers, yet as a rule, there seems to be a connection between
professional performers and the spiritual side of life. Many pros
draw tremendous energy and power from a deep faith in a greater
force. In recent years, many who were turned off by fear-based
organized religions in their childhood have turned to new-thought
churches and centers, such as Unity and Science of Mind. Whatever the source of their spiritual faith, world-class performers do
tend to hold strong spiritual convictions.

▶ ACTION STEP FOR TODAY

Take inventory of the ten people closest to you. On a scale of 1
to 7, 7 being the highest, how much faith do these people have
in themselves? How much faith do they have in a higher power?

Odds are that your level of faith is the average of these ten people. Ask this critical thinking question: "Is this helping me or hurting me?"

50

Champions Handle Fear
Like A Snake Charmer

" 'Come to the edge,' He said. They said, 'We are afraid.' 'Come to the edge,' He said. They came. He pushed them . . . and they flew."

– Guillaume Apollinaire, 1880-1918, poet

The relationship performers have with fear is a significant distinction between amateurs and professionals. Amateurs are controlled by their fears, while professionals learn to embrace fear, like a snake handler holding a venomous king cobra by the neck. Champions know if they get sloppy or stop paying attention, the cobra will take their life. The great ones use the energy and intensity of fear to drive them to greater heights. They learn how to become comfortable while performing in an uncomfortable state of mind. Repeated exposure to their fears systematically desensitizes them, eventually depleting the fear. An interesting phenomenon often occurs after this desensitization process – performers fall in love with the activity they used to fear. Suddenly, they can't get enough of the activity, because it makes them feel so good. Since the beginning of public opinion polls, the number one fear among people worldwide has always been public speaking. The fear of public humiliation is too much for the ego to bear; so most people develop a tremendous fear of speaking to groups. Realizing the incredible force public speaking can be in their careers, many champions have faced this fear head-on and later fell in love with the emotional high public speaking offers. Champions have learned emotional strength and power lies on the other side of fear. On the other end of the spectrum, amateurs usually settle for the short-term gain of avoiding what they fear.

▶ **ACTION STEP FOR TODAY**

Take inventory of your fears: are they adult fears, or adolescent fears? An adult fear is being afraid of a truck about to run over you. It's the kind of fear that can save your life. Adolescent fear is being afraid of the bogeyman under the bed, or of being rejected by a prospect or embarrassed in front of a group. The threat is literally made up in our minds. When we allow adolescent fear to hold us back, we are behaving like children.

51

The Great Ones Evolve From Fear To Love Based Motivation

"Everyone has two choices. We're either full of love. . .or full of fear."
— *Albert Einstein*

Middle-class performers are mediocre because they have failed to identify the emotional motivators that burn from within. Upper-class performers are full of emotional fire that is usually fueled by the fear of failure. While fear can be a tremendous motivator, it creates a lot of pain and suffering in the process. Operating out of a fear and scarcity based consciousness is a playing not to lose strategy, and through the law of attraction acts as a magnet for additional thoughts of fear and scarcity to enter the performers mind. These thoughts eventually manifest more fear and scarcity on the physical plane. The upper class includes some of the most successful people in the world, who are also some of the saddest. The fear that propels them to achieve is the same emotion that robs them of their fulfillment. The upper class consciousness is rooted in ego, where the pain of losing is stronger than the pleasure of winning. Because of the fear this thought process attracts, the upper class tends to suffer much more than the world class. As soon as they succeed at whatever they are attempting, they are on to the next conquest, and the victories must get bigger for them to sustain their ego-based gratification. The world class transcends this lower vibration by focusing their thoughts, language, and mental pictures on love and abundance. The great ones are playing to win, and winning to them simply means learning and growing. They literally transcend the addiction to feeling superior to anyone else, and for being afraid to lose what they have. Their dominant thoughts are on their vision for the future, and they pursue it fearlessly.

▶ **ACTION STEP FOR TODAY**

Ask these critical thinking questions: Am I more motivated by my fear of failure or by the excitement of my vision? Am I out to prove myself or express myself?

52

Champions Understand
The Limits Of Money

"When you're doing something you love to do, the only
reward you need is the experience of doing it."
— *Bill Gove, 1912-2001, the father of professional speaking*

In pursuit of happiness, amateurs tend to seek riches, while pros seek fulfillment. The irony is that champions create so much value in their quest for fulfillment that they often develop substantial riches. Amateurs are usually looking for the quick buck. They believe being rich will fill the hole they feel inside, although few of them can say how much money that would require. In truth, no amount is sufficient, because the hole can only be filled by feelings of fulfillment. The great ones find fulfillment in their everyday work and activities. They never really chase fulfillment, yet they experience it simply by doing their work. Amateurs believe money and the things money will buy are the keys to peace and fulfillment. Professional performers gravitate toward things that create a sense of satisfaction in and of themselves. Fulfillment is a mental state champions experience as a result of their elevated awareness. In essence, champions invest the necessary time and resources to discover what they love to do and then focus on doing it to the best of their ability. Their fulfillment doesn't come from the results of their actions, but from the actions themselves. The great ones are focused on the cause, rather than the effect. As a result, the effects (or results) take care of themselves. On the other end of the spectrum, the masses are focused on the effects, and often ignore the causes. Even if they succeed in acquiring money and possessions, fulfillment continues to elude them, until they finally throw up their arms and say; "Is this all there is?" The answer is yes, because money and material possessions are effects, and effects don't create causes. Causes create effects. This is why the pros seek fulfillment first though loving what they do for a living. This is a can't-miss strategy. Their work creates a tremendous sense of fulfillment – even if the effects aren't reached. Champions don't play for the money; they play because they love the game itself. The money – the effect – is just icing on the cake.

▶ ACTION STEP FOR TODAY

Do a cause-and-effect analysis. Ask this critical thinking question: "Am I focused on the cause of my fulfillment, or the effect of my fulfillment?" For example, do you exercise for the health benefits you gain, or because you love the sport or exercise activity?

53

Champions Are Future-Oriented

"All great leaders have vision and idealization in which they can continually imagine the perfect outcome to all situations."
— *Brian Tracy, author and speaker*

While amateurs often live in the past, champions look toward the future. Pros habitually focus on the present while creating their ultimate vision for, and landscape of, the future. This future orientation allows them to dream of grand visions and unlimited possibilities. It also keeps them motivated and moving forward by keeping the proverbial carrot out in front. Amateurs like to talk about the good old days, and how they wish things were like they were before. Professional performers are just the opposite. The pros revere and respect the past, but place responsibility for the future squarely on their own shoulders. Taking personal responsibility for failures, successes and actions in general is a trait of world-class performers. The saying, "If it is to be, it is up to me," reflects their beliefs. Average people would rather see themselves as victims of circumstances beyond their control. The great ones make their own circumstances and respond with a higher level of awareness to negative events in their lives. Their execution-based focus and future orientation keeps them on track. It all begins with taking full responsibility for their lives and their futures.

▶ **ACTION STEP FOR TODAY**

Program yourself by repeating this statement until you believe it: "The past is only important as it relates to the present and the future, and any mistakes in my past have been for the purpose of helping me create a bountiful future." This affirmation harnesses the power of the past and directs it to the only place it can serve you: in the future.

▶▶▎ **WORLD-CLASS RESOURCE**
Listen to Create the Future: How to Think Big, Act Bold, and Be a Visionary, by Bill Gove, Larry Wilson, Bob Proctor and Steve Siebold. You can find it at www.govesiebold.com

54

The Great Ones Challenge The Facts

"When the dream is big enough, the facts don't count."
— *Ray Youngblood, entrepreneur and speaker*

Most progress relies on professional performers who stand up, challenge the status quo and push the envelope. The great ones definitely dance to the beat of a different drummer, and I thank God they do. Many great breakthroughs and innovations are made by champions who ignore the facts and figures. While amateurs are content with the status quo, pros are always seeking a better, faster, more efficient, effective method or way of doing things. The great ones derive incredible pleasure from ongoing growth and development, while amateurs quietly fear change will create more demanding or less pleasurable conditions. To amateur performers, champions can appear to be outrageous in their wants and desires. Amateurs are accustomed to the way things are, and prefer to keep it that way. Without champions, innovation and progress would be almost nonexistent. At the beginning of the 20th century, many scientists believed every major innovation and invention had been discovered. This type of thinking is difficult to sell to pros, who tend to listen only to other pros. While champions take facts into consideration, they just don't allow them to carry as much weight as amateurs do. The great ones know progress relies on the unreasonable men or women who stand up and challenge the facts, and then take intelligent action to exceed them.

▶ **ACTION STEP FOR TODAY**

Begin to question the so-called 'facts' governing your life. Ask these critical thinking questions: "Is it a fact that it's going to take me 20 years to retire? Is it a fact that I will gain weight as I get older or after having children? Is it a fact that the only religious beliefs I should follow are the ones handed down from my parents?"

55

Champions Are Driven By Fun

"When you have confidence, you can have a lot of fun, and when you have fun, you can do amazing things."
— Joe Namath, professional football player

One of the most closely-held secrets of world-class performers is how much fun they have in what they do. Outsiders see big-time performers as super self-disciplined, self-sacrificing, success-and-achievement machines. Yet a closer look gives a more accurate portrayal of what really drives these people: fun. Champions have more fun in their work than any other group. They take whatever time is necessary to choose a career path that encompasses their natural talents, abilities, and, most of all, their passions. Amateurs have a difficult time competing with pros because most amateurs hate their jobs — one of the primary reasons they're amateurs in the first place! Professional performers are highly disciplined, of course, yet their core drive and mental fortitude seem to come from the pure fun, excitement, enjoyment and exhilaration of their work. Average people go to work and plod through the day; champions go to work and have fun. This is one of the reasons amateurs cannot compete with pros – it's a mismatch from the start. One is focused on surviving, while the other is just playing a game and having fun.

▶ **ACTION STEP FOR TODAY**

How much fun are you having in your life? On a scale of 1 to 7, 7 being the most fun, give yourself a rating in each area of your life. Next, ask this critical thinking question: "Can I eliminate doing things that aren't fun?" Really think about your answer. Life is short and unpredictable. Why do things you don't enjoy unless it is impossible to escape them?

56

The Great Ones Learn To Forgive

> "The weak can never forgive. Forgiveness
> is the attitude of the strong."
> – *Mahatma Ghandi, 1869-1948, Indian leader*

Professional performers' heightened awareness allows them to forgive freely. While average people plot revenge, champions release their enemies and move on. The amateur approach stems from ego; the professional approach from spirit. The habit of forgiveness is a significant distinction between the masses and the champions. Professional performers understand that mental toughness and power ultimately come from a mindset of love – love for what they do, who they are and for the people with whom they interact. This is not to be confused with the Age of Aquarius and the free love movement of the 1960s, although they were probably on the right track in the beginning. All human actions and reactions have their root in one of two forms of consciousness: fear or love. If people were primarily logical creatures, this concept wouldn't make sense. Human beings, however, are primarily emotional creatures who often operate in irrational ways.

Champions know this, which is the reason they're able to forgive. Emotional creatures who operate at a lower level of conscious awareness tend to say ignorant things and behave in thoughtless ways. Expecting human beings to behave logically all the time is like expecting machines to feel emotion. The great ones operate from a love-based consciousness that recognizes the emotion-based irrational behavior of people. Champions are much more forgiving than average people because of this knowledge.

▶ **ACTION STEP FOR TODAY**

Make a list of all of the people you feel have slighted you to some degree, and give yourself the gift of a lifetime by forgiving them. You don't have to tell them you forgive them; simply forgive them in your heart by coming to terms with the fact that we are fallible human beings doing the best we can.

▶▶**ı WORLD-CLASS RESOURCE**

To learn more about the power of forgiveness, get a copy of Forgiveness: How to Make Peace with Your Past and Get on with Your Life, by Dr. Sidney Simon.

57

Champions Know Why They Are Fighting

"One of the hallmarks of the great ones is their level of awareness as to what they are willing to fight for. They're willing to suffer and sacrifice to make their visions reality."

– Steve Siebold

Average performers never fully tap into their own psyches, and as a result, they are unmotivated to dream big dreams. World-class performers know what they are willing to fight – and even die – for. This is a critical trait of the great ones. They draw their motivation and willpower intrinsically, whereas the middle class waits for the motivational mood to strike. Professional performers invest a tremendous amount of time thinking about what makes them tick in an effort to uncover their deepest, most powerful emotional motivators. When the going gets tough and the pain kicks in, average people back off from a goal or task. This is when the world class really begins to fight. When they begin to feel physical or psychological pain, they go inside themselves and draw on their vast reserves of emotional power. When pain strikes, the subconscious mind asks the conscious mind, "why must I suffer?" The great ones know the answer is their vision. When their subconscious determines the vision is worth fighting and suffering for, their level of motivation soars. This is one of the major reasons there is such a chasm between amateurs and pros. The difference may be small at the start, but as the pain and suffering escalate, the performance gap becomes larger and larger, to the point of a total mismatch. You don't pit amateurs against pros. It's like feeding a man to the lions.

▶ ACTION STEP FOR TODAY

Make a list of the ten reasons you will do whatever it takes to breathe life into your vision. Review this list every day, especially when the going gets tough.

▶▶❘ WORLD-CLASS RESOURCE

Get a copy of It's Not About the Bike, by Lance Armstrong. This book will take you inside the mind of the greatest cyclist in history. After you read it, you'll know exactly what makes this champion so special.

58

Champions Know Very Good Is Bad

"The mental toughness process is not about going from good to very good--it's about going from good to great. Anyone who settles for very good is destined to spend their golden years bathed in a sea of regret, wondering why."

— Steve Siebold

The world class controls over 90% of the wealth in America for a simple reason: they are competing in a marketplace full of amateurs. The only group that has a fighting chance against the great ones is the upper class, which represents approximately 10% of the population. At Mental Toughness University, we classify most members of the upper class as 'Very Good Performers'. In order to ascend to the world class, performers must be classified as 'Great'. At the highest levels of performance, very good is considered to be bad. There are lots of performers who are very good, but great performers are rare. At the height of my tennis career, I was a very good player, but compared to the world class, I was bad. Very good performers are no match for the great ones. The difference between a very good leader and a great leader is the respect and loyalty of his/her team. The difference between a very good doctor and a great doctor can be life and death. The difference between a very good salesperson and a great salesperson is financial freedom. For the average person, to be classified as very good is something to be proud of. For the great ones, it's an insult. Both groups have the same potential. The only difference is in their thinking.

▶ ACTION STEP FOR TODAY

Ask this critical thinking question: Are you a good performer, a very good performer, or a great performer? For the correct answer, check the results you've been getting in each area of your life up until this point. Your self-assessment represents the truth. Your results represent the fact.

59

The World Class Embraces Free Enterprise

"That some should be rich shows that others may become rich, and hence is just encouragement to industry and enterprise."
– Abraham Lincoln, 1809-1865, U.S. President

The free enterprise system in America has created more great champions than anything else in the history of civilization. Since the world class operates from a fearless state of abundance, they tend to embrace the free enterprise system. Many great ones cut their entrepreneurial teeth in the corporate world and then launch a business. Some choose to become professional performers within the corporate structure. These champions make the shrewd decision to use the collective knowledge, power and systems of their billion-dollar employers. They don't relish the recognition and gratification of being in business for themselves; they prefer to flourish and grow within the corporate system. While most rank-and-file employees are more interested in where they're going on vacation than in moving forward in their career, the great ones often think of the company as their own. The free enterprise system lives within them. Every move they make serves the company for which they work. These performers are a rare breed, especially in times when the masses believe their companies have no loyalty to them. This sense of distrust gives middle-class performers an excuse to coast. The great ones are aware that their performance and work ethic are about them, not the company.

World-class performers are always reinforcing the habit of excellence – one of the reasons they will always be in demand in any economy.

▶ ACTION STEP FOR TODAY

Commit to seeing yourself as self-employed, regardless of who signs your paycheck. Employment status is unimportant in the Age of the Mind. All of us are the presidents of our own professional services corporations, and lease our time and efforts to employers or customers. This mindset should motivate you to perform to the best of your ability every single day.

▶▶I WORLD-CLASS RESOURCE

Read How to Get Rich, by Donald Trump.

60
Champions Believe In Global Citizenship

"Without a global revolution in the sphere of human consciousness, a more humane society will not emerge."
— *Vaclav Havel, Czech Republic president*

The world class believes in the philosophy of one collective global economy. This is evident by their participation in such groups as Rotary International and others that focus on assisting people globally. True champions know what happens in Bombay affects what happens in Chicago, and what happens in Sydney affects what happens in Tokyo. Average people hardly know their own neighbors. The middle class seldom looks beyond their own hometowns and tends to have an isolationist philosophy. They are not any less caring than their world-class counterparts; they are simply unaware of the impact countries and people have on each other. With their expanded global worldview, professional performers create ideas that usually have no geographical boundaries.

The World Wide Web has expanded this awareness even more, yet the middle class fails to embrace this philosophy as a whole. Until more people raise their level of awareness, the great ones will have to foot the bill for everyone. The end of mediocrity as we know it doesn't seem to be anywhere in sight.

▶ **ACTION STEP FOR TODAY**

Ask these critical thinking questions: "Am I a global citizen? Am I actively contributing to people and places outside where I work and live?" Set a goal to elevate your participation in global problem solving by helping someone in need in another country in some way.

61

The Great Ones Don't Give Back . . . They Just Give

"Don't give back . . . just give."
– Nido Qubein, author, speaker, philanthropist

World-class performers usually have a strong philosophy when it comes to giving. Middle-class consciousness is rooted deeply in fear, but world-class consciousness is rooted in love and abundance. Professional performers tend to have a world view that there is, and always will be, more than enough of everything to go around. As a result, they tend to give freely. People operating at poverty-, working-, and middle-class levels of awareness will give from time to time, yet there is a difference. They tend to give in order to get. In other words, people at lower levels of awareness often see giving as a trade. It's an "I give you this, so you have to give me that," mentality. The great ones give without reservation or anticipation of a trade. They give because they believe it's the right thing to do, and as a result, they experience much deeper levels of fulfillment than average people. World-class performers are not more generous; they simply believe they'll never run out of resources and that the world operates from total abundance. Giving is easy when you believe the source of supply is unlimited. The world-class mindset is pure love, with no beginning, no end and no limits. The amateur-class philosophy demands that all giving be measured, for fear the fountain will run dry. As a result of this subtle distinction, the world class gives more, gets more, and attracts more.

▶ ACTION STEP FOR TODAY

Give money to someone who needs a few bucks, without any expectation of receiving anything in return. Maybe it's the guy begging for money on the street, or possibly a friend in need of some fast cash. This habit manifests a prosperity consciousness that will attract more abundance into your life.

▶▶I WORLD-CLASS RESOURCE

Check out my mentor in the area of philanthropy, Nido Qubein, at www.nidoqubein.com. He's quite a guy.

62

The World Class Is Obsessed With Their Goals

"There is one quality which one must possess to win, and that is definiteness of purpose, the knowledge of what one wants, and a burning desire to possess it."
– Napoleon Hill, 1883-1970, author

Average performers set their goals on New Year's Eve and don't look at them again until the next New Year's Eve. The world class is in a constant goal-setting mode. Champions are goal-setting machines – they know the cornerstone of all achievement is mental clarity. Professional performers are evolving so rapidly they usually find it necessary to review – and sometimes reset their goals on a daily basis. One of the secrets of their success is this daily exposure to their goals. Only 3% of Americans have clearly defined written goals, and less than 1% can identify their primary goal and objective in life. This attention to detail gives the great ones an incredible advantage over their middle-class counterparts. As average performers begin to forget what their goals are because of a lack of exposure to them, the pros are imbedding their goals deep into their subconscious minds daily. Their minds are like guided missiles, always adjusting and correcting to maintain accuracy toward the target. Champions have a singleness of purpose most people will never take the time to discover, and this thought process allows them to climb higher every day.

▶ ACTION STEP FOR TODAY

List your ten major goals for this year every morning when you wake up. This habit will ingrain your major goals into your psyche. This is one of the most important habits you can develop enroute to a world-class mindset.

▶▶ **WORLD-CLASS RESOURCE**

Read Goals! How to Get Everything You Want – Faster Than You Ever Thought Possible, by Brian Tracy. This book takes a no-nonsense, no-holds-barred approach to setting world-class goals.

63

The Great Ones Believe They Cannot Fail ... They Can Only Learn And Grow

"Growth itself contains the germ of happiness."
– Pearl S. Buck, 1892-1973, author

Champions are committed to never-ending personal and professional growth. Average performers believe learning and growing begins and ends in school. The world-class ranks realize graduation is the beginning of the road, not the end. Professional performers attempt so many things over the course of their lifetimes that their mental growth rate is staggering compared to the masses. While amateurs avoid risk at any cost, the great ones are always looking for opportunities. They are willing to fail their way to success. The belief of the champion, according to author Larry Wilson, is "I cannot fail... I can only learn and grow." This belief makes pros very dangerous performers. While average people attempt to win while simultaneously trying to avoid pain, champions give it the full-court press with little or no concern about failing. Champions have programmed themselves to disengage their fear and move full speed ahead. The middle and lower class are amateurs at failing; they are so afraid of it they only attempt goals they know they can reach. The feelings of bliss that champions experience don't stem from their successes, but from the fulfillment of the growth that occurred along the way.

▶ ACTION STEP FOR TODAY

Begin telling yourself you cannot fail; you can only learn and grow. Keep repeating these words to yourself at every opportunity for the next 30 days, and see what happens. You will create a new world-class belief that may transform your life.

64

Champions Are World-Class Communicators

"When dealing with people, remember that you are not dealing with creatures of logic, but with creatures of emotion."
– Dale Carnegie, 1888-1955, author

Champions know that one of the most critical factors for success is their skill in dealing with people. Average performers know this as well, yet while the masses attempt to communicate and influence people through logic, the great ones know human beings are emotional creatures masquerading as logical creatures. Based on this information, champions tweak their approach. The crown jewel of champion-level success with other people is knowing a critical factor in human relations – helping people fulfill their insatiable desire to feel important. From doctors to bus drivers, emotional creatures crave validation and acceptance . . . and professional performers know it. As a result, their conversations are peppered with language that makes others feel important. In business, average workers converse for personal satisfaction. The great ones converse to influence and persuade others to see their unique point of view.

▶ **ACTION STEP FOR TODAY**

Go out of your way to make everyone you speak to feel important. A good start is remembering names in conversation. Make this a daily habit and watch how people begin to respond to you.

65

Champions Are Products Of Their Habits

"We first make our habits, and then our habits make us."
– John Dryden, 1631-1700, author, playwright

Average performers think of habits as something to break, like smoking or eating too much. Professional performers know successful habits are the keys to the kingdom. Each and every day, the great ones reinforce their success habits, such as exercise, proper diet, showing up early/staying late, and studying their field. Champions have a sacred respect for the power that habits exhibit in their life. The pros know if they allow their championship habits to slip for even one day, the habit will begin to atrophy. The great ones know it's more difficult to develop a championship habit than to lose it. They understand the magnificent force of momentum can work for or against them. As a result, they tend to protect their success habits with an almost religious fervor. Champions are keenly aware of how their habits impact every area of their lives, because they always look inside themselves and listen for answers. Average people are oblivious to success-habit formation, unless the pain from an unhealthy habit becomes too great. Habits are the raw materials from which the great ones are made.

▶ **ACTION STEP FOR TODAY**

Make a list of five habits that could lift you to higher levels of success and fulfillment. Now, select the single habit that would have the most impact and make a commitment to make it a part of your life. Remember, it takes an average of three to four weeks to form a new habit, whether it is positive or negative.

▶▶I **WORLD-CLASS RESOURCE**

Read The Seven Habits of Highly Effective People, by Stephen Covey.

66

The Great Ones Understand The Power Of Humility

"If anything goes bad, I did it. If anything goes semi-good, we did it. If anything goes really good, then you did it. That's all it takes to get people to win football games for you."

– Paul 'Bear' Bryant, 1913-1983, legendary football coach

While average people never consider the magnitude humility plays in the ability to solicit help from others, the pros have reverence for it. Professional performers know humility is one of the most effective approaches ever created to influence people. The case for humility, even for the best performers, is easily made. Even members of the world class stumble and fall many more times than they succeed. Humility is the natural order of the human condition, yet average people walk around clouded by ego and false pride. This is undoubtedly costing them dearly in relations with others. A braggart is essentially saying, "I'm better than you." That's not a good approach to a species who craves the feeling of importance. Champions recognize the damage done through boasting, and adopt an attitude of gracious humility. The champion's self-confidence is no less than a braggart's. As a matter of fact, all of the pros I've ever known have what I call inner arrogance. The difference: they don't display this arrogance outside their own thought process. This supreme confidence is necessary to compete at the world-class level, but pros know how to conceal this well-earned, positive sense of self.

▶ **ACTION STEP FOR TODAY**

Ask this critical thinking question: "On a scale of 1 to 7, 7 being most humble, how humble do you appear to other people?" If you scored less than 7, make a commitment to raise your score by at least one point right now by becoming more aware of how you appear to others. Start by moving from an ego-based consciousness to a spirit-based consciousness. Begin this process by making a list of ten things for which you are most grateful. Next, express gratitude to people in your life who have helped you succeed. Notice how this humble, spirit-based consciousness begins to attract and positively impact the people around you . . . not to mention the impact it will have on you.

▶▶❙ **WORLD-CLASS RESOURCE**

Read *Attitudes of Gratitude*, by M.J. Ryan

67

The World Class Achieves Happiness From Being And Becoming, Not Acquiring And Possessing

"The human spirit needs to accomplish, to achieve, to triumph, to be happy."

— Ben Stein, author and actor

While average people are on a psychological manhunt for happiness, the world-class ranks recognize that happiness cannot be pursued directly. The great ones know happiness is a byproduct of living life to the fullest. The pros forget chasing happiness and turn their attention to fulfilling the vision they have carefully constructed. Happiness eludes the masses because they haven't invested the time and energy to study the animal. The masses repeatedly attempt to create happiness from the outside in, whereas the great ones know sustained happiness stems from being and becoming, not acquiring and possessing. Average people have mastered short-term happiness, easily gained through instant gratification mechanisms such as eating, spending money, or engaging in any pleasurable activity. The world class invests a substantial amount of time insuring their future happiness by creating congruency between who they are, what they're doing, and where they're going. Champions are masters at doing such things as marrying the right person, selecting jobs they love and building friendships with people they admire and respect. As a result, they indirectly develop an incredible sense of gratitude and happiness.

▶ ACTION STEP FOR TODAY

Ask this critical thinking question: "If you could be, have and do anything you wanted, what would that look like?" Write or type a one-page essay describing your answer. Forget any self-imposed or perceived limits. Write this essay as if anything were possible.

▶▶I WORLD-CLASS RESOURCE

Read The 100 Simple Secrets of Happy People, by David Niven, Ph.D.

68

Champions Believe In Honesty

"It is possible that the scrupulously honest man may not grow rich so fast as the unscrupulous and dishonest one; but the success will be of a truer kind, earned without fraud or injustice. And even though a man should, for a time, be unsuccessful, still he must be honest: better to lose all and save character. For character is itself a fortune."

– Samuel Smiles, 1812-1904, physician, author

Champions pride themselves on being honest, open and straight-forward. They carry these philosophies into everything they do, and are unwilling to sacrifice them. While some people acquire wealth dishonestly, professional performers know real success lies in who you become, as opposed to what you acquire. The great ones focus their efforts on becoming the kind of people who can attract the things they want out of life. Some amateur performers believe success can be acquired (even if it's done dishonestly) and will manifest feelings of happiness. Average people have a lottery-like mentality, which explains why the lottery is so popular. The lottery mentality is not dishonest, but it carries the premise that more money and material possessions automatically lead to being happier and more fulfilled. The great ones have learned the real victory is what they become as a result of the struggle. Removing the struggle removes the victory. If honesty is removed, the richness of the achievement is diminished.

▶ **ACTION STEP FOR TODAY**

Commit to purge your life of dishonesty. The external effects of dishonesty are crippling to your reputation; the internal effects are deadly to your soul.

69

The World Class Knows Great Ideas Are The Solution To Success

---

"The ideas I stand for are not mine; I borrowed them from Socrates. I swiped them from Chesterfield. I stole them from Jesus. And I put them in a book. If you don't like their rules, whose would you use?"

– Dale Carnegie, 1888-1955, author

Ideas are the business champion's primary asset. They have the power to alter the world for the better. Average people greatly underestimate the potential value of their own ideas. Professional performers know money will flow from any idea that solves a problem, and the bigger the problem, the richer the payoff. Champions cultivate their own ideas and the ideas of other world-class performers. The great ones are always engaged in critical thinking as it relates to problem solving, and as a result, treat ideas with the respect they deserve. Amateur performers tend to dismiss many ideas before they have a chance to be properly evaluated and tested. When things get tough, the masses turn to others for help. When times get tough for champions, they turn their attention to the inner workings of their minds so they can capture and cultivate great ideas that can help turn things around. Average performers turn to outside sources when money gets tight, but the great ones get quiet and focus on their thoughts and feelings, looking for ideas on how to raise money fast. Most people never take their ideas beyond the talking stage, but if champions believe in the idea, they move to the next step without hesitation.

▶ **ACTION STEP FOR TODAY**

Commit to treat your ideas as if they were the children of your soul . . . because they are.

70

The Great Ones Are Products Of Their Own Imagination

> "The great, successful men of the world have used their imaginations...they think ahead and create their mental picture, and then go to work materializing that picture in all its details, filling in here, adding a little there, altering this a bit, but steadily building, steadily building."
> – *Robert Collier, 1885-1950, author*

While average performers think of imagination as child's play, the world class relies on it as a mental preview of things to come. Before champions make a move, they have lived out the scenario through imagination. The great ones know imagination is the first step in the design of the perfect house or the perfect life. Through this powerful faculty, they can preview their futures. Champions often go on sabbaticals to places of great natural beauty for the sole purpose of heightening their sense of imagination when pursuing the solution to a problem. Pros understand the power of their creative mind, and strengthen their imaginative skills by drawing on them daily. The masses are oblivious to this awesome natural gift. Champions combine the power of imagination with their penchant for action, and the results are the stuff of which dreams are made. While the middle class is scolding their children for daydreaming and letting their imaginations run, the great ones are impacting the world with the manifestation of their visions. As the Aborigines are fond of saying, the world class is literally "Dreaming their world alive."

▶ **ACTION STEP FOR TODAY**

Commit to investing three minutes each day reviewing the essay you wrote in Action Step 67. Allow your imagination to run wild with ideas of your perfect life. Remember to ask this daily question: "If there were no limits, what would I be, have, and do?" Forget about the 'how-to' part of the equation during this exercise, and suspend any disbelief you may have. This three-minute daily habit has the power to transform your life forever.

71

Champions Don't Let Feelings Get In Their Way

"It's easier to act your way into good thinking than it is to think your way into good action."

– Bill Gove, 1912-2001, the father of professional speaking

People operating at the poverty-, working-, and middle-class levels of awareness are always getting ready to get started toward their goals. The poverty class is going to find work soon; the working class is getting ready to move up from night shift to day shift; the middle class is going to start working on that graduate degree one of these days. All have good intentions; yet they rarely move beyond their intentions. They are always waiting and wondering when the time will be better for them to begin. They are waiting for their emotions to motivate them to action, and as a result, they become slaves to their feelings. Champions are masters of their emotions, and they know that waiting to feel like taking action is a losing proposition. They believe there is never a better time to get started than today, and that tomorrow is merely a promissory note; that any day could end up being their last. The great ones operate with a keen sense of urgency, dreaming of the future while firmly rooted in the present. Average people are smart enough and gifted enough to make their dreams come true, yet tend to wait so long to attempt anything substantial that, by the time they have failed enough to have learned the lessons they need to succeed, their life is over. Professional performers have a heightened sense of life's timeline, and their actions reflect. While the masses are waiting for the mood to strike them to act, the great ones start acting, regardless of whether they feel like it or not. This small distinction in their thought process makes the difference between living their dreams and dying with their music still inside them.

▶ ACTION STEP FOR TODAY

Decide to develop the habit of not leading your feelings get in your way. Make a commitment to get started today, and continue the commitment for the next thirty days, regardless of whether you feel like it or not. Remember, habits start out as cobwebs and turn into cables.

▶▶▎ WORLD-CLASS RESOURCE

Purchase a copy of Bill Gove's Golden Gavel Acceptance Speech at www.govesiebold.com. This 39-minute speech on DVD is one of the funniest and most insightful presentations you'll ever see. In this talk, Bill addresses how most people let feelings get in their way and keep them from doing the things they want to do.

72

The World Class Operates From Love And Abundance

"Life in abundance comes only through great love."
– Elbert Hubbard, farmer, author

Average performers never consider the broad scope and significance love has on everything we do. Professional performers know we can only operate from one of two frames of consciousness at any given time – ego or spirit. Middle-class performers are masters of operating from ego, in which pride and self-righteousness are the objectives of the game. Amateur performers believe their success is primarily their own doing. They believe in the self-made man/woman theory. The world class is aware that all good things come from the spirit of love. They know love is the natural order of the universe, and that ego and self-pride have been created by man over the centuries to cover a fragile self-image. Many people feel inferior to others and mask their feelings by displaying false pride and bravado. The great ones embrace love as the root of their success and feelings of fulfillment. They know that without the loving guidance and support of others, they could not have reached or even dreamed of aspiring to the world class. Their recognition of and gratitude for the power of love creates more abundance in their lives. This fountain of potential continues to bless the champions. The only thing that can clog the system is ego, which is the evil stepchild of fear. The great ones lock the door when ego comes to town. They only acknowledge the spirit-based consciousness, which they recognize by its calling card: love and abundance. Ego cannot exist in this realm, only gratitude. While the amateur egotistically believes he is responsible for his great success, the pros know that the abundance of life comes from a far greater source.

▶ ACTION STEP FOR TODAY

Monitor your mental state of mind. Ask this critical thinking question every couple of hours: "Am I operating from a consciousness of ego, or a consciousness of spirit?" The answer is the blueprint of your behavior. Your approach to problems, people and life is greatly influenced by your operating state of mind. The world looks very different through the spirit than through the ego.

▶▶I WORLD-CLASS RESOURCE

Read The Science of Mind, by Ernest Holmes.

AM I OPERATING FROM SPIRIT OR EGO?

The Spirit is . . .Non-judgemental • Loving • Accepting • Tolerant • Devoid of pretension • Calm • Abundant • Friendly • Win/Win • Forgiving • Self-less • Creative

The Ego is . . .Judgemental • Fear driven • Afraid of risk • Competitive • Pretentious • Rushed • Scarce • Friend-less • Win/Lose • Unforgiving • Selfish • Frustrated

73

World-Class Leaders Are Willing To Get Fired Everyday

"Any great leader or coach has to be willing to put it all on the line. You have to be willing to be fired every day when it comes to standing up for what you believe in."
— *Billie Jean King, tennis legend and coach*

Amateur thinkers make lousy leaders because they operate out of a fear-based consciousness. Fear-based leaders succumb to politics and pressure, which cripples their ability to lead. Professional thinkers operate out of love and abundance and fearlessly lead their people to become more than they ever believed possible. The most common commodity in corporate America is the sales manager who craves the approval and friendship of his sales team. This manager is more interested in making friends than developing champions. The second most common commodity is the sales manager who rules her team with an iron fist, refusing to consider feedback or input from the field. Both of these managers are performing out of fear, and are both a dime a dozen. The world-class leader is neither dictator nor baby sitter. Great sales leaders have only two objectives: drive sales and develop people. Sometimes that means being unpopular and pushing people beyond their comfort zones, and other times it means being there for a team member who has hit rock bottom. World-class leaders are chameleons who are able to change and adapt to any situation, always with the same goal in mind: bringing out the best in the people they lead. Sometimes that means being tough. Other times it means being tender. Championship leaders are always walking the razor's edge, and are willing to take any risk necessary to achieve their objectives, even to the point of being fired. The great ones never play it safe when it comes to leading their team through change, knowing their job is to serve as a guide and coach to their teams. World-class leaders follow their values and beliefs and lead boldly and fearlessly. If their leadership costs them their job, the pros know they can write their own ticket and work for any company they choose. The welcome mat is always out for the great ones.

▶ **ACTION STEP FOR TODAY**

If you're a leader, manager or coach, ask these critical thinking questions:

1) Am I leading, managing, or.....coaching out of love or fear?
2) Am I more concerned about.....being liked or leading people?
3) Do I have the courage to be.....a strong, progressive leader..... who brings out the best in.....people?

74

Champions Don't Care Who Gets The Credit

"Knowledge is power, which is why people who had it in the past often tried to make a secret of it. In post-capitalism, power comes from transmitting information to make it productive, not from having it."

– Peter Drucker, consultant

Average performers believe information is the key to whatever success they've had, and they tend to hoard it for fear of losing their power. Champions are different. Champions know that information is everywhere. The secret is taking action on the information and developing competence. Middle-class performers are stuck in the mindset that knowledge is power, when the truth is that intelligent use of knowledge is and always has been the seat of true power. Pros are information-sharing conduits for their organizations. Because they are working from a spirit-driven, instead of ego-based mindset, who gets the credit makes no difference. Amateurs are afraid that, if they don't get the credit often enough, they will be forced out of their companies. Every decision to share information is carefully considered by amateurs. The pros operate from abundance; fear is the last thing on their minds. Creating dynamic, positive feedback loops is an ongoing mission for the champions. In their roles as leaders, they have driven fear out of their organizations. People are encouraged to challenge ideas and information for the good of the organization. The great ones know that if sharing too much information ever costs them their position, they are always in demand in the marketplace. The pros will always share information and credit, and will always be able to write their own ticket.

▶▶ı ACTION STEP FOR TODAY

Rate your willingness to share information for the good of the organization on a scale of 1 to 7, 7 being most willing. If you score less than a 5, you may be operating primarily from an ego-based consciousness rooted in fear. Make a commitment to shift your thinking more toward your spirit self.

75

Champions Are Zealots For Change

"The people who get into trouble in our company are those who carry around the anchor of the past."
– *Jack Welch, former chairman and CEO, General Electric*

Average performers hold on to skills, competencies, and mindsets that have gotten them to the position they hold today.

Champions know business and technology are changing so rapidly that constant innovation is the only way to thrive and survive. While average performers are addicted to the methods and strategies of the past, pros know that, by the time most products hit the shelves, they are nearly obsolete. The world they were trained to succeed in during school no longer exists and the rules keep changing. Amateurs struggle to keep things the same, while pros embrace change at all levels and learn to thrive on it. Middle-class performers see change as a threat; world-class performers see it as the most exciting time in human history. The great ones know constant innovation is the order of the day. They always look for a better way. As a result, greater innovation collectively leads to more rapid change. Professional performers see all of this as a game in which the individual who can be the most open, flexible and innovative wins. Average people yearn for the good old days. The great ones know these are the good old days.

▶ ACTION STEP FOR TODAY

Identify another old belief, strategy or idea from the past that is no longer working in the present, and make a commitment to update or dismiss it. In the age of the mind, knowing when to make room for new ways of getting results is critical to your success.

▶▶◁ WORLD-CLASS RESOURCE

Read Making Change Happen One Person at a Time, by Charles H. Bishop Jr. This book is an excellent resource for accessing the change capacity of any organization. For seminars and consulting, check out Chicago Change Partners at www.chicagochange.com

76

The Great Ones Operate With Integrity

"In looking for people to hire, you look for three qualities: integrity, intelligence, and energy. If they don't have the first, the other two will kill you."
— *Warren Buffet, CEO, Berkshire Hathaway*

While operating from a mindset of fear and scarcity, average people tend to view integrity as a luxury they hope to be able to keep. In their effort to survive in a world they believe is out to get them, integrity often gets left behind. Pros have the advantage of operating from love and abundance, which dictates that integrity be the baseline of every action taken. Champions have a reputation for total integrity; it is the foundation of their entry into any playing field. The great ones are always welcomed. Their co-workers, colleagues and contacts know that when push comes to shove, champions will always do the right thing. Integrity is a habit of the pros, not because it succeeds, but because it's the right thing to do. When a champion tells you he will do something, you can take it to the bank. Their handshake is a binding contract. Contrary to what they teach in business school, handshake deals are still very common among the world class. The great ones play by different rules, and rule number one is total integrity.

▶ ACTION STEP FOR TODAY

Just for today, operate with complete integrity. Do every single thing you promise yourself and others. Experience what it's like to operate like one of the great ones. A word of caution: you may become addicted to the results you achieve through this experience!

77

The Great Ones Are Bold

"Only the bold get to the top."
– Publilius Syrus, 1st Century B.C., writer of Mimes

Champions, in general, are a bold group of people. Their superior self-confidence allows them to constantly push the envelope. Where average people are afraid they will not be liked or respected by others, champions are only concerned with whether their efforts will impress their mentor teams and their networks of contacts. Average people appear lazy to champions, so their opinions and ridicule don't hold much weight. The downside of world-class boldness is brazenness – when boldness is simply taken too far. Champions are so laser-focused on their targets and objectives that they can push too hard at times. This is when their mentor teams become the eyes and ears of the performers and get them back on track. The great ones are always pushing. Boldness is so prevalent in champions because their belief system keeps telling them they're getting close to victory, and a little more effort will do the trick. What average people see as being pushy, champions see as part of the price for success. It's a small nuance in thinking that leads to very large results.

▶ ACTION STEP FOR TODAY

Just for today, be bolder than you've ever been, and see how it feels. Give your fears a day off and pretend it's impossible to fail. At the end of the day, record your thoughts and feelings about this exercise for future reference.

▶▶I WORLD-CLASS RESOURCE

Read The Art of the Deal, by Donald Trump. The billionaire real estate tycoon reveals his boldness throughout this fascinating book, and will give you ideas about how you might apply boldness to different aspects of your life.

78
Champions Are Interdependent

"If we are to compete effectively in today's world, we must begin to celebrate collective entrepreneurship – endeavors in which the whole of the effort is greater than the sum of the individual contributions. We need to honor our teams more, our leaders and maverick geniuses less."

– Robert Reich, former U.S. Secretary of Labor in the Clinton administration

Average people tend to view the thoughts and ideas of others not only as potentially useful, but also as threatening to their egos and existence. As a result, amateurs are severely limited in the size and scope of their accomplishments. Champions understand the world is an interdependent, complex network in which the aggregate potential is limitless. The pros don't need to ride off into the sunset as heroes. They prefer to tackle bigger ideas and accomplish more by working with a team of like-minded, high-integrity, world-class individuals. Ross Perot said it well: "Life is more like a cobweb than an organizational chart." The great ones know successful people and organizations of the future must rely on the collective collaboration of the team. With this in mind, the pros embrace and celebrate the contributions of all team members. The amateurs feel threatened by the group, and set out to insure they are properly credited by their superiors. The great ones do the exact opposite. They want to insure individual team members receive enough credit for their contributions without being overshadowed by people in more visible roles. The difference creates a phenomenon known as "ferocious cooperation."

▶ **ACTION STEP FOR TODAY**

Ask this critical thinking question: "Am I an independent leader looking for recognition, or an interdependent leader looking for achievement without being concerned about who gets the credit?"

79

The World Class Knows The Leader's Primary Role

"Leadership is not a designated position; it's a phenomenon. It is people following people because they want to, not because they have to."
– Larry Wilson, founder, Wilson Learning Corporation

Average performers see the leader as an authority figure who has the power to hurt them. As a natural result of this fear, amateurs focus on staying out of their leader's line of sight, hoping to avoid trouble. Champions embrace leadership for what it is: the facilitation, guidance, and influence necessary to bring about change. The pros know leadership, at its highest level, is facilitated by example. While average people view leadership as a role, the great ones know the heart and soul of leading goes well beyond the title or position. The pros know a leader's role only creates a limited amount of influence. They know leadership is dependent on gaining the respect and admiration of a group of people who independently decide to follow. Leadership is bringing out the best in people for the common good of the organization, and placing the credit where it honestly belongs: with the team. The pros see leadership as building a team, connected both intellectually and spiritually, in order to manifest the vision of the unit. It is a humbling and awesome responsibility. Champions are grateful for the opportunity to bring about change and evolve as individuals at the same time.

▶ **ACTION STEP FOR TODAY**

On a scale of 1 to 7, 7 being the highest, how would you rate yourself as a leader? Ask three people who know you well to rate you on the same scale. With brutal honesty, ask them to explain why they rated you as they did.

▶▶❙ **WORLD-CLASS RESOURCE**

Get a copy of Leading Change, by John P. Kotter.

80

A World-Class Attitude Leads To World-Class Happiness

"I have a one-word definition of attitude: life. Attitude is the difference maker in life. It's the treasure that lies within you. A positive attitude is the key that jump starts your life. Attitude dictates whether you're living life or life is living you. Attitude determines whether you are on the way or in the way."

– Keith Harrell, speaker and author

World-class performers all seem to agree that attitude is everything. Our research shows some champions are more focused on attitude than others. While two people might be at the same level of success, the one more focused on attitude reports being happier. While the masses try not to have a bad attitude in their struggle to survive, champions have a positive attitude and always try to improve their mental approach to life. While average people view the idea of attitude as fluff and rah-rah motivation, the world class sees it as the cornerstone of life. They realize their attitude has an impact on everyone they meet and everything they do, as well as a monumental effect on their level of happiness and fulfillment. At some point, champions realize the self-fulfilling nature of their own mental approach to life, and make a decision to talk themselves into the attitude they wish to have. With this in mind, it would make sense that the higher ups in any organization have better attitudes. In our research, we found this to be true in most cases. Yet our research disclosed something I believe is even more profound: the better the attitude toward life, the happier people seemed to be. This proves the old idea that we create our own sense of happiness, regardless of our station or lot in life.

▶ ACTION STEP FOR TODAY

Do a quick test: On a scale of 1 to 7, 7 being best, how good is your attitude toward life? Use critical thinking and be honest. If you score less than a 7, remember that attitude is a decision, and you can upgrade your world view at any time. Attitude is a perception, created in our minds, that has little or nothing to do with circumstances, events or other people. It is the foundation of all of our habits, actions and behaviors.

▶▶❙ WORLD-CLASS RESOURCE

Invest in your attitude by reading or listening to the man known in corporate America as Dr. Attitude, Keith Harrell. You can find his books and CDs in any major bookstore or by visiting www.keithharrell.com

81

Champions Seek Balance

"There is more to life than increasing its speed."
– Mahatma Ghandi, 1869-1948, Indian leader

Average people don't really have an issue with balance, because they are not fully engaged in their work. Balance is the Achilles' heel of world-class performers. In a perfect world, the world-class could strike the perfect balance between work, leisure, and life. In reality, the great ones are embroiled in a constant struggle to maintain a balanced life. Average performers think their life is out of balance if they work after 5 p.m., pull a night shift once in a while, or work on a weekend. They want the same luxuries the world class enjoys yet are unwilling to work for those luxuries. They will swear this isn't true, but the proof is in the pudding. Middle-class mentality creates middle-class results. The numbers never lie. Average people live a life of self-deception and quiet desperation, yet argue their life is out of balance because they work so hard. The pros have the opposite problem. They burn the candle at both ends, and usually need more rest and recovery time than they allow themselves. Some of the great ones have mastered balance, but most walk a thin line between over-achievement and under-relaxation. As one of them admitted to me recently, "Yeah, I do struggle with balance, and I'm working on it. But on the other hand, I'd rather burn out than rust out." The masses err on the side of too much leisure, while the world class errs on the side of too much work. If you had to bet every cent on one of them being successful and happy, who would you put your money on? Your answer says a lot about which group you inhabit.

▶ ACTION STEP FOR TODAY

On a scale of 1 to 7, 7 being most balanced, how balanced has your life been during the past six months? Make a commitment to add or subtract one activity that would increase your score by at least one point.

▶▶I WORLD-CLASS RESOURCE

The best speaker I've ever heard on the subject of life balance is Polly Bauer, the former president of the Home Shopping Networks Credit Corporation. Visit her website, www.speakerpollybauer.com

82

Champions Are Professional Listeners

"Listen to everyone in your company, and figure out ways to get them talking. The folks on the front line – the ones who actually talk to the customers – are the only ones who really know what's going on out there. You'd better find out what they know."

– *Sam Walton, 1919-1992, founder, Wal-Mart*

Amateur performers underestimate the power of listening. In conversation, while others are talking, they're thinking about what they're going to say next. The pros are very different. They see listening as the key factor in uncovering what is really going on inside the minds of other people. Human beings are emotional creatures, with a driving need to be understood, yet 95% of us aren't listening. The champions understand this need and use it to connect with people on an emotional and spiritual level. World-class salespeople know listening to the needs of the prospect is the single most important thing you can do in the sales process. World-class managers know questioning and listening to their sales people are the most effective methods of getting to know what motivates and moves them to action. The great ones practice listening in meetings, at cocktail parties and anywhere else they can hone their skills. Professional performers have a profound respect for the art of listening and they use this skill to help them achieve their goals.

▶ ACTION STEP FOR TODAY

Strike up a conversation with someone and see how long you can keep that person talking. Practice listening at a higher level. Ask for clarification and for repetition of information. Try to get a sense of what this person is really feeling. Make a game out of getting good at listening.

▶▶ WORLD-CLASS RESOURCE

Read Deep Listening, by Robert Haskell, Ph.D.

83

The Great Ones Are Masters Of Momentum

"Momentum producers understand an important law of physics: 'Objects at rest have no momentum.' They know the power of their thinking, planning and acting. Bottom line -- momentum producers are hard to stop."

– David Pollay, founder, The Momentum Project

The masses are oblivious to the magnitude of the role momentum plays in the performance of emotional creatures. The world class knows an emotional creature on a hot streak can become a champion if the momentum lasts long enough. Momentum is a state of mind that ignites energy, enthusiasm and passion. A professional salesperson who thinks he is 'in momentum' sounds and acts like a different person. In fact, emotionally speaking, he is a different person. The great ones use momentum to fuel their passion and transfer their beliefs to others. Professional performers learn to control their emotions and create the perception of momentum before it technically exists. The great ones know if the perception of momentum is present, confidence and power will continue to increase. While average people stumble into momentum from time to time, world-class performers create this emotional thought process from scratch. Momentum is a subjective emotional perception, and therefore can be manufactured in the mind. This artificial creation attracts more momentum, until world-class performers are rolling forward like a locomotive. The major distinction: average people wait for momentum to strike. The great ones create it on demand.

▶ ACTION STEP FOR TODAY

Keep repeating this: "I have massive momentum." Find different ways to program yourself with this message until you begin to believe it. Remember, the subconscious mind cannot make the distinction between what is real and what is vividly imagined. Use the power of language to talk yourself into an emotional state of momentum toward your goals.

84

World-Class Achievement Requires Teamwork

"What is the recipe for successful achievement? To my mind, there are just four major essential ingredients: Choose a career you love . . . Give it the best you have in you. Seize your opportunities . . . And be a member of the team."
– Benjamin Fairless, 1890-1962, former president, U.S. Steel

World-class performers learn to see their greatest achievements as a team effort. They realize grand achievements demand more than any one person can deliver. They enlist other great performers to join the team, and often give most of the credit for their achievements to these talented team members. They have graduated from the ego-driven stage of the self-made man/woman theory, realizing that there is no such thing. They love the admiration for their achievements, yet are more than happy to share the kudos with their teammates. This shared work/credit philosophy allows champions to take on big projects with bold vision. When they approach an opportunity, they think of the talent they will have to assemble to be successful, with little or no thought of who will get the credit for their success. Their world view of achievement seems to be, "It takes a village." In some cases, champions are the team leaders, yet they are willing to be subordinates if it serves the best interests of the project and/or makes the most sense strategically. In the minds of champions, hard work and achievement are the building blocks of a successful and happy life.

▶ ACTION STEP FOR TODAY

Create a dream list of the ten people you would most like to serve on your team. Next to each name, list the reasons you selected that person. Make this list even if you don't have a major project in mind. The simple act of identifying these people will set off a series of thought processes that will lead you to the perfect project for this team.

▶▶I WORLD-CLASS RESOURCE

Experience The Great Game of Life, a high performance team-building and corporate culture development course by Larry Wilson. www.greatgameoflife.com

85

Champions Evolve From Proving Themselves To Expressing Themselves

"The ego-driven middle class and upper class are out to prove themselves. The spirit-driven world class wishes only to express themselves. One struggles against the current while the other floats peacefully down the river."

– Steve Siebold

Amateur performers are often driven by a need to prove themselves to themselves and other people. This need can easily become an addiction for a person who craves acceptance and validation from the outside world. Professional performers evolve to a higher level of consciousness where outside approval is no longer necessary. Champions still enjoy the accolades and acceptance of people they respect, but are no longer motivated to take action to achieve this acceptance. The great ones are often motivated through self-expression, by the need to share their unique talents and abilities with the world. Abraham Maslow, the father of humanistic psychology, said it this way: "In order for human beings to reach self-actualization, they must become all they can be. The writer must write. The painter must paint. The salesperson must sell." The world class doesn't do these things to please other people, gain notoriety or get rich. They do it because it expresses who they are to themselves. In essence, champions learn who they are in the act of self-expression, and often choose to share themselves with the world. The act of proving oneself is based in ego and rooted in the fear of not being good enough. The act of expressing oneself is based in spirit and rooted in the love of wanting to share and celebrate a person is uniqueness and inner beauty. Proving oneself is a process that must be forced onto others because of the attachment the performer has to the outcome. Expressing oneself is a natural process that has no attachment to anything or anyone. The more praise they get, the more they need to feel good about themselves. Expressing oneself creates feelings of fulfillment in the act itself, regardless of any outcome. It's one of the reasons the great ones are more mentally tough than their amateur counterparts.

▶ **ACTION STEP FOR TODAY**

Ask this critical thinking question: Are you out to prove yourself or express yourself?

86

World-Class Managers See Themselves As Change Agents

"Good management consists of showing average people how to do the work of superior people."
– John D. Rockefeller, 1839-1937, founder, Standard Oil

Managers with a middle-class consciousness believe their job is to maintain order and keep things on course. Managers operating with world-class consciousness believe their job is to bring about change. The difference between the two philosophies is profound. One is a babysitting service; the other, a leadership role. Managers who are emotional amateurs see themselves as gatekeepers and guardians to the people in the field. They are a buffer between the people on the front lines and the executive suite. Managers who are emotional professionals see themselves as change agents in a quintessential transformational position. One is a job; the other is a career. One brings out the best in people; the other maintains the status quo. The great ones are part motivator, coach, counselor, parent, planner, negotiator and psychologist. Most of all, the best ones lead by example with their attitudes and actions. Their actions are mirrored by their team, and they set the tone. When managers are world class, you can bet their people are not far behind.

▶ ACTION STEP FOR TODAY

If you manage or lead, ask this critical thinking question: "Do my actions reflect a manager or a leader? Am I more interested in bringing about change or in maintaining the status quo?"

▶▶ı WORLD-CLASS RESOURCE

Every world-class manager should have a copy of this classic book: Maslow on Management, by Abraham Maslow. This may have been the most important work of one the finest minds of the 20th century.

87

Champions See Mistakes As Intellectual Capital

"The trouble in America is not that we are making too many mistakes, but that we are making too few."
– *Phil Knight, founder and chairman, Nike*

Mistakes are viewed as failures by amateur thinkers. The aggregate cost of workers hiding their mistakes out of fear of reprisal runs well into the billions of dollars each year. Professional thinkers see mistakes in a totally different light. They see mistakes as a company asset, to be recorded and duly avoided in the future. The real cost is not the mistake itself, but in the lack of reporting and recording the mistake so it could be avoided in the future. The great ones know the only way to avoid making mistakes in business is to stop coming up with new ideas. The pros embrace mistakes; they are a sign the organization is pushing forward and forging into uncharted waters. Champions know the secret to mistake management is to drive the fear of reprisal completely out of the organization. They reward people for sharing their mistakes with the entire company, so the mistakes will not be repeated. The great leaders know the future belongs to the individuals and organizations which can bring about and adjust to rapid change in a permanent white water world, while simultaneously encouraging the team to open up and share both failures and successes.

▶ ACTION STEP FOR TODAY

Encourage your subordinates to share mistakes with you and your team. Reward them for being forthcoming. On a scale of 1 to 7, 7 being most progressive, how progressive are you when it comes to mistake management? If you scored less than 5, make a commitment to drive the fear of reprisal out of your organization. It's most likely costing you a fortune.

88

The Great Ones Only Negotiate Win-Win Deals

"My father said, 'You must never try to make all the money that's in a deal. Let the other fellow make some money, too, because if you have a reputation for always making all of the money, you won't have many deals.'"

– J. Paul Getty, 1892-1976, founder, Getty Oil

When it comes to the art of negotiation, there are two basic approaches. The amateur thinker sees negotiation as a competition between two parties to see who can get the better end of the deal. This mindset is rooted in ego, as opposed to spirit, with little or no consideration for the other party. The professional thinker is different. She operates from spirit; her goal is to come to terms that benefit all parties. A champion doesn't see negotiations as a battle of wills, but as a method of reaching a mutually beneficial agreement where all parties walk away satisfied. A pro has a reputation for honesty, fairness and compassion, and typically refuses to enter into any kind of business deal or arrangement with people who don't also exhibit these qualities. A world-class performer rarely does business with people outside the world class; it's an unwritten law. Champions prefer to do things in a very straightforward manner. Anyone who violates this trust finds himself ostracized. The unspoken rules of negotiation are simple: be fair, and make it a win-win deal. A champion knows every symbiotic negotiation opens the door to more business. More importantly, a champion lives and does business according to one major philosophy: do the right thing.

▶ ACTION STEP FOR TODAY

Ask these critical thinking questions: "Do I negotiate to get as much as I can, or do I look for the win-win deal? Do my business colleagues see me as a smart and shrewd negotiator, or as a smart negotiator who does the right thing?" In the age of an interdependent, seamless, global economy, the future belongs to the smart and compassionate negotiator.

▶▶ WORLD-CLASS RESOURCE

Get a copy of The Secrets of Power Negotiating, by Roger Dawson. This six-hour audio album will give you a master's degree in negotiation skills. Visit www.rdawson.com

89

The World Class Builds And Nurtures An International Network Of Contacts

"If I had to name the single characteristic shared by all truly successful people I've met over a lifetime, I'd say it is the ability to create and nurture a network of contacts."

– Harvey Mackay, founder, Mackay Envelope Corporation

The average person sees networking as attending business and social events, passing out and picking up business cards. While this is a legitimate forms of networking, the world class operates on a higher level. Champions know the most valuable assets they have are their personal and professional networks. In business, you can measure the power of a player by the size of the Rolodex. Politicians are the greatest networkers on the planet. Every time they land in a different town, they call the most influential business leaders in the area who are in their network, just to say hello. They are tirelessly developing, building and maintaining relationships with the most powerful people they can reach. Professional performers are not only collecting business cards, but also hand-picking exactly who they want to network with, based on who can help them the most. World-class performers know most of the people who attend networking events are people hunting for business. They want to invest time networking with other members of the world class, so they strategically place themselves in world-class settings such as fund raisers, benefits, political functions, and country club outings. While the middle class collects business cards at rubber chicken dinners, the great ones build relationships with the movers and shakers of society. The difference in strategy is profound, and requires something only the world class possesses: supreme self-confidence. The middle class sees this as a crass operational strategy of using people to climb the ladder of success. The world class sees it as a symbiotic, synergistic relationship of give and take. Friends do favors, grant privileges and create opportunities for friends. It's the emotional nature of man to want to help people who have helped him. The great ones are on a never-ending quest to develop opportunities to reach out and assist people in their network. Then, when they need help, there's a psychological debt to which world-class performers respond. The power of contacts has put more than one president in the White House and into other powerful positions. It is possible for the average person to literally propel herself into the world-class ranks by constructing a powerful network of contacts and friends. Of course, the middle class is surrounded by the same opportunity every day, yet choose to let it pass in lieu of some other activity where effort is minimal and pleasure is king.

▶ ACTION STEP FOR TODAY

Make two separate lists of contacts. The first list is your Top 100. This list consists of the 100 most powerful people you know, who will return your phone calls. The second list is called the Dream 100. This list consists of the 100 most powerful people who you would love to have on your Top 100. Set a goal to convert as many people from your Dream 100 to your Top 100 as possible over the next 12 months. Remember that (most likely) the only thing standing between you and your ultimate vision is the help and support of enough other people. One contact can literally change your life.

▶▶I WORLD-CLASS RESOURCE

Pick up a copy of How to Build a Network of Power Relationships, by Harvey Mackay. This two-hour CD is jam-packed with tips and suggestions you won't hear anywhere else.

90

The Great Ones Never Hesitate To Seize Opportunity

"The lack of opportunity is ever the excuse of the weak, vacillating mind. Opportunities! Every life is full of them . . . every newspaper article is an opportunity. Every client is an opportunity. Every sermon is an opportunity. Every business transaction is an opportunity – an opportunity to be polite, an opportunity to be manly, and opportunity to be honest – an opportunity to make friends."

– Orison Swett Marden, 1848-1924, founder, Success Magazine

Amateur performers are perpetually waiting for their ships to come in. They're waiting for the man on the white horse, singing, "Here I come to save the day!" The masses seem content to wait to inherit their fortune from some long-lost rich relative or by winning the lottery. The casinos are full of amateurs, looking for opportunities. The pros don't view opportunity as something to wait for, but as something they create for themselves. The more opportunities that the world class creates, the more that seem to come their way. The great ones know they are completely responsible for how their lives turn out. Average people keep hoping luck and circumstance will favor them. Meanwhile, the champions are out impacting the world. At the heart of this difference in philosophy is a lack of fear. The great ones are unafraid to fail at a new opportunity. They see opportunity as a game that must be played now, while there is still time left on the clock. If they fail at that game, they move on to a new game. They just keep playing until they win. Amateurs are so paralyzed by the fear of losing that they never get in the game. As a result, they never develop the courage and confidence to play at the world-class level. Security, to the middle class, is much more important than seizing opportunity. But like happiness, security cannot be sought directly. Security is an illusion created by the masses to justify not taking risks and fulfilling their potential. The great ones play the game and capitalize on every opportunity until the end. Meanwhile, the amateurs come to the end of their lives and arrive safely at death.

▶ **ACTION STEP FOR TODAY:**

Make a list of the five biggest opportunities you are considering taking advantage of, and make a decision to move forward on at least one of them in the next 24 hours. Suspend any fear you may feel during the decision-making process and take a calculated risk. Building this habit is a necessary prerequisite to ascending to the throne of the world class, and the only way to develop this skill is by doing it.

91

Champions Are Masters Of Mental Organization

"In organization there is always strength. Especially is this true in regard to a well-organized human being. He doesn't waste his substance, but is forever improving his mind and giving and radiating confidence."
– *George Matthew Adams, 1878-1962, author*

A key trait of the world class is their ability to determine what they want, why they want it, and how to get it. They are mentally organized and this shows up in every aspect of their performance. Average people wallow around, unclear about what they want and unsure if they are competent enough to get it. Instead of disciplining themselves to organize their thought processes, it's easier to lose themselves in things like television, booze, drugs, and other destructive and pleasure-based activities. Amateurs are smart enough to know they should create an organized plan for their life, but opt to be distracted by outside activities. Thinking, real thinking, may be the hardest work of all. The world class invests a substantial amount of time planning, creating and revising their strategy to manifest their ultimate vision. While average people spend more time organizing and planning their yearly vacation, the great ones are structuring and restructuring their lives daily. Professional performers know their mind is a moving river, making new inroads every day, and therefore requires never-ending revision of their ultimate goals and dreams. No matter what stage of the game they're in, the great ones are conscious of the value of ongoing mental organization and clarity of purpose.

▶ ACTION STEP FOR TODAY

On a scale of 1 to 7, 7 being most organized, rate your mental organizational skills. In other words, rate your level of mental clarity, starting with the vision for your life all the way down to scheduling your daily activities. If you score less than a 5, it's time to revisit the vision you have for your life. After you establish a clear vision for where you want to go, your daily organizational skills and priorities will become self-evident.

92

The World Class Catapults Their Consciousness By Overcoming Obstacles

"The block of granite which was an obstacle in the path of the weak, becomes a stepping-stone in the path of the strong."
– Thomas Carlyle, 1795-1881, author

While the masses see obstacles as their primary adversary, champions view them as opportunities to expand their level of thinking and competence. Professional performers know the only way they can truly become mentally tough enough to manifest their vision is to struggle and fight their way through obstacles. There is no other way. The great ones are conscious of the fact that success is trial by fire. The middle-class consciousness avoids obstacles at all costs and looks for the easy way out. The world class builds their own roads and forges ahead, knowing the strength of character gained from overcoming obstacle after obstacle will be the measure of their true success, and with that rock-solid character, even greater things can be accomplished. If you remove the obstacles, you remove the opportunity to grow. The world class becomes great by overcoming more obstacles than the middle class. They get tough because they're in the game, getting hit and taking shots. Professional performers are good at overcoming obstacles because they are always engaged in this process. Amateurs spend so little time staring down the dragon that they simply never get tough enough to become pros. The fear of failure looms deep in the psyche of the masses. The great ones are sometimes fearful, yet develop more courage with each new obstacle, until they stand up one day as true mental warriors.

▶ **ACTION STEP FOR TODAY**

Make a list of the three biggest obstacles you currently face. Next, determine the worst thing that could possibly happen if you decided to mount an all-out assault to overcome them. If you can live with the worst-case scenario, suspend your fear and attack your obstacles as if it is impossible to fail. If you succeed, your self-confidence will soar. If you fail, you will live to fight another day.

93

The Great Ones Are At Peace With Themselves

"The foundation of mental toughness is to always be at peace with yourself."

— Jerry Zimmerman, tennis coach

Amateur performers tend to believe peace of mind can be sought and captured. Professional performers know chasing after peace guarantees it will elude them. Peace, much like happiness, is an elusive state of mind, reached only when performers have done everything within their power to achieve or accomplish a task or goal. The peace of mind experienced is an indirect result of knowing that all possible physical and mental resources have been exhausted in the process. Average performers are all too aware they are not giving it 100%, so peace of mind continues to elude them. Instead of increasing their efforts, they usually decide to employ a distraction of one form or another to avoid thinking about their half-hearted efforts. The great ones are like old warhorses: they keep coming back for more. Professional performers either win the game and experience the exhilaration of victory, or they suffer defeat with the peace of mind of knowing they did everything in their power to win. It's a winning proposition either way. The world class is at peace with themselves because they understand the laws of human nature.

▶ ACTION STEP FOR TODAY

Ask these critical thinking questions: "Am I at peace with myself? Am I satisfied with who I am as a human being? Do I feel I am enough just being who I am, or do I define myself by my successes and failures?" Be honest with yourself, and then make a commitment to bring more peace into your life. Remind yourself that you already have everything you need to be at peace with yourself. You were born with it, and your greatest successes and worst failures can't ever change this universal truth.

▶▶I WORLD-CLASS RESOURCE

Read Notes to Myself, by Hugh Prather. This little book will have you contemplating the idea of peaceful thinking in a whole new way. It's a philosophical classic.

94

Champions Know The Power Of Persistence

"If I had to select one quality, one personal characteristic that I regard as being most highly correlated with success, whatever the field, I would pick the trait of persistence. Determination. The will to endure to the end, to get knocked down seventy times and get off the floor saying, "Here goes number seventy-one!"

– Richard M. DeVos, founder, Amway Corporation

Average people never truly decide what they want, so they wander from job to job, chasing different things until time finally runs out. Persistence, to amateurs, is never really a factor, because they haven't focused on any single goal long enough to be persistent. When pros determine what they want, they burn their vision into their minds on a daily basis. They become obsessed with attaining the goal at almost any cost. At this stage, persistence becomes the primary factor in their success. Amateurs are often impressed by this, yet the champions are simply following their passions and refusing to look back. They reach a mental state in which the failure to persist is no longer an option. The great ones know the longer they hang tough, the greater the odds of victory. What looks like Herculean persistence to the outside world is really just the manifestation of world-class mental clarity in action. Champions decide what they want, down to the last detail, and then wage war to get it. Their sense of purpose and dogged persistence is a hard combination to beat. The great ones become unstoppable because they've convinced themselves there is no way to fail. This subjective perception is one of the most common thought processes of the world class. While the rest of the world watches with doubt and disbelief, champions talk themselves into believing that winning is their destiny and defeat is impossible. This winning expectation is the fuel that drives the champion to persist until they succeed, no matter how much pain they have to endure.

▶ ACTION STEP FOR TODAY

Make a list of the times you exhibited iron-clad persistence. Go back to your childhood, if necessary. Next, ask this critical thinking question: "If I applied that same world-class persistence to my current challenges, would it change my life?" If the answer is yes, you know what to do!

▶▶I WORLD-CLASS RESOURCE

Read the 1921 classic, The Go-Getter, by Peter Kyne. This book is the ultimate tale of a man who refused to settle for second best. I guarantee it will alter the way you think about the concept of persistence forever.

95

The World Class Pursues Power To Manifest Their Dreams

"You all have powers you've never dreamed of. You can do things you never thought you could do. There are no limitations in what you can do, except the limitations in your own mind as to what you cannot do. Don't think you cannot. Think you can."

– Darwin P. Kingsley

Average people have no idea how powerful they can be. The masses tend to believe only the rich and famous have power. Professional performers have a clear understanding of their personal power, as well as their power to influence, inspire, motivate and persuade other people. The world class wants to become more powerful for the purpose of expanding their influence. Amateurs who develop or acquire power can be lethal weapons. If you want to see the true character of a man, give him power. Power tends to bring forth the innate nature of the person, much like alcohol does. Feed some people a few drinks too many, and they become belligerent and mean. Power has the same effect. On the other hand, grant power to the pros, and they will use it for good. The response to the power stimulus stems from character. Champions use power to help themselves and to help other people, without becoming attached or addicted. The great ones know all power is temporary; the only purpose it serves is to help and liberate people. Only the great can possess power and not abuse it. While the masses tend to view powerful people as evil, arrogant and greedy, the world class knows it's how power is used that makes it good or bad. The ego-driven upper class tends to use power as a tool of manipulation. The spirit-driven world class uses the same power to help set themselves and other people free. Power in the hands of egocentric leaders is dangerous. Power in the hands of the great ones is what's responsible for the growth and success of civilization.

▶ ACTION STEP FOR TODAY

Ask this critical thinking question: "Do I wield my power from an ego- or spirit-based consciousness?" Make a conscious effort not to abuse people with your power. Remember, the abuse of power is a manifestation of the ego in action. If you make the shift to a spirit-based consciousness, this elevated level of vibration will keep you focused on using your power for the greater good of all. This habit of operating from a spirit-based consciousness also creates feelings of love and abundance that lead you to believe in your limitless potential, as well as the limitless potential of others. This phenomenon occurs when your spirit is vibrating at the same frequency as the force that created the universe. It's like tuning into a radio station: the sound only gets clear when you tune into the frequency of the radio signal.

96

The Great Ones Always Push For Progress

> "Progress consists largely of learning to apply laws and truths that have always existed."
>
> – *John Allan May, author*

The masses tend to rebel against change and progress. It makes them feel uncomfortable because it's unfamiliar. They perpetually long for the good old days, although you sometimes get the feeling they were doing the same thing then! The pros know progress is the way of the world; it needs to be embraced and supported at every turn. In recent years, the gap between amateurs and pros has widened because of the rocket-like acceleration of progress in business and in life. The great ones think progressively and talk almost exclusively about the future. Their philosophy seems to be, "Onward and upward." While most people are complaining about how things are never going to be the same, champions are applauding the same concept. They know things are not supposed to be the same; that progress is the natural order of a healthy, growing society. Amateurs feel victimized by progress. It scares them. The fear and scarcity they carry inside themselves is saying, "What if I'm not good enough to survive in this new environment?" Meanwhile, the world class is saying, "Bring it on!"

▶ ACTION STEP FOR TODAY

What is your attitude toward progress? Do you react to progress with fear or do you respond to progress with love? Just for today, adopt an attitude of love and abundance toward progress of any kind, even if you have to fake it. Tell yourself and others how thrilled you are about the progress that's taking place. Become aware of how this makes you feel. Remember, you can always go back to a fear-based consciousness. The masses are afraid of almost everything, and they would prefer that you feel the same way. After a day of thinking and speaking thoughts of love and abundance, it will be up to you whether to go back and join them, or to forge ahead with a new or upgraded world-class attitude toward progress.

97

Champions Praise People Lavishly And Often

"Appreciative words are the most powerful force for good on earth."
– *George W. Crane*

A mateur performers tend to see praise as a luxury, to be passed on sparingly to others from time to time. Champions use praise as an integral component in their everyday interactions with others. Most people are literally starving for praise, due to the fact that 95% of the population are amateurs in the art of inter-personal communication. Emotional creatures have a high need, and some even a mild addiction, to the sweet-sounding words of encouragement and recognition. Professional performers are care-ful not to praise the same person too often for fear of diminishing the power of their words. At the same time, they actively search to catch people doing something that merits carefully thought-out and well-spoken words of kindness. Champions know a little praise goes a long way in making people happy. An honest compliment might be remembered for years to come. Kind words cost nothing, yet accomplish so much. World-class performers know all doors open to praise and courtesy, and more significantly, all hearts open, too. The great ones use praise to lighten the load, ease the burden, and warm the heart. They know most people are lonely, afraid or suffering through some kind of painful situation that's invisible to the rest of the world. Champions are a beacon of light in a cloudy, stormy, unpredictable world. Armed with praise, they are the ultimate force for good.

▶ ACTION STEP FOR TODAY

Make a commitment to become a 'Praise Finder,' always looking for praiseworthy behavior to reward with words. Once this world-class habit becomes a part of your everyday consciousness, be aware of the impact it has on your relationships with others. When dealing and communicating with other people, remember most of us are starved for praise, no matter how high a position we occupy.

98

The World Class Is Always Willing To Pay The Price

"I am wondering what would have happened to me if some fluent talker had converted me to the theory of the eight-hour day and convinced me that it was not fair to my fellow workers to put forth my best efforts in my work. I am glad that the eight-hour day had not been invented when I was a young man. If my life had been made up of eight-hour days, I don't believe I could have accomplished a great deal. This country would not amount to as much as it has if the young men of fifty years ago had been afraid that they might earn more than they were paid for."

— *Thomas Edison, 1847-1931, inventor*

The average person would be flabbergasted at the amount of time and effort that professional performers invest on their way to the top. Amateurs use words like lucky and opportunistic to describe the world class, but they couldn't be farther from the truth. The great ones pay a tremendous price for their success. While the masses spend an inordinate amount of time planning and scheming ways to avoid doing the work necessary to win, champions are out on the playing field paying the price. The middle-class consciousness is convinced there is a shortcut to success, and are bound and determined to find it. Of course, there never has been a shortcut to success, nor is there a glamorous method of paying the price. There is only the blood, sweat and tears of delayed gratification. There is only the pain and suffering of practice. There is no escape from it, and the winners know it. You either pay the price for success or pay the price in regret. Only champions know the price of success is a much lighter burden to bear than the ongoing torture of regret. As speaker Jim Rohn says, "Paying the price weighs ounces . . . but regret weighs tons." To thinking and contemplative people, the only intelligent choice is paying the price. The alternative is mental torture. Success is a toll road . . . pay now or pay later. You already know what the great ones do.

▶ **ACTION STEP FOR TODAY**

Ask this critical thinking question: "Do my current habits, actions and behaviors suggest I am more interested in instant pleasure or delayed gratification?" If the answer is instant pleasure, don't feel bad. 95% of the population falls into this category. If you're ready to break free of the pleasure loop that leads to regret, decide today to begin pursuing the path of delayed gratification. This doesn't mean you can't enjoy pleasure. Just focus on tasks, activities and goals that will give you gratification for a lifetime, instead of just a few minutes.

99

The Great Ones Are Aware Of Their Limitless Potential

"Compared to what we ought to be, we are only half awake. We are making use of only a small part of our physical and mental resources. Stating the thing broadly, the human individual thus lives far within his limits. He possesses power of various sorts which he habitually fails to use."

– *William James, 1842-1910, author*

People operating at the poverty-, working- and middle-class levels of conscious awareness seem to be governed by beliefs which keep them bound to a life of quiet desperation. Because most of us inherited and learned our beliefs from well-intentioned amateurs, it makes sense that the majority of us are convinced we can only go so far in life. Champions know this to be a colossal myth that has held millions of people in a mental prison. By the time most people figure out they've been sold a bill of goods, their lives are nearly over. The most common regret mentioned by residents in nursing homes is, "I should have tried more things and taken more risks." The world class either receives professional-level programming as children or is lucky enough to be exposed, mentored or influenced by one of the great ones along the way. The latter is far more common. Champions wake up one day and realize their possibilities and potentials are almost limitless. They realize if they are willing to pay the price, they can build a mentor and support team that can help them accomplish nearly any goal or dream they can envision. After this realization, only a small percentage of people actually take the next step – deciding on the single thing they want more than anything else. This will be the primary focus and driving force of their lives. Most people fall by the wayside because they simply want too many things half-heartedly. The great ones make a decision, build a team and shake the world.

▶ ACTION STEP FOR TODAY

Ask five people who really know and care about you to give you a list of your five greatest attributes and talents, and why they believe you are so gifted in these areas. You may be surprised at how others perceive you, and these lists may inspire you to tap some of the talents that you didn't even realize you had. Be sure to make a copy of these lists and put the originals in a safe deposit box or some other safe place. These lists will be a source of motivation and inspiration for you for the rest of your life, especially during times of doubt and despair.

100

Champions Prepare To Win

"The flinch factor…when not prepared to win we will flinch
when the customer poses a question we cannot handle."
— *Lou Wood, Region Business Director, Johnson & Johnson/OMP*

Average people seem to have a strategy of "Ready, fire, aim!"
In other words, most people fail to do the necessary preparation and planning it takes to succeed. Middle-class performers
have a fondness for winging it. Some actually brag about their
lack of planning, like a kid in school who boasts about not studying for an exam. Amateur performers are always looking for the
easy road, yet appear to be confounded by their lack of success.
Champions are perennial planners. They are always charting and
changing their course to be certain everything is on track. Skating
the details of preparation never occurs to the world class, because
they are surrounded by a society full of amateurs who prove the
theory doesn't work. The great ones don't limit their plans to their
own scope of knowledge and experience. They know someone,
somewhere, knows how to do it better and is willing to help. Planning isn't popular with amateurs because it's not always fun and it
rarely produces instant pleasure. The masses are professional pleasure seekers and planning doesn't fall into this category. Champions have learned to delay their gratification as long as necessary in
order to breathe life into their goals and dreams.

▶ **ACTION STEP FOR TODAY**
Commit to creating a ninety-day action plan to carry you closer
toward your ultimate vision for your life. Ninety days is long
enough to build momentum and short enough to keep your
attention. Toward the end of this time, create another ninety-day

action plan. This habit is one of the best practices of Fortune 500 sales and management teams.

101

The World Class Is Committed To Personal Development

"I've spent the last forty years trying to convince corporate America that the fastest way to improve the bottom line was in the personal development of their employees."

– Larry Wilson, founder, Wilson Learning Corporation

Average performers wouldn't read a personal development book or listen to a personal development recording if you paid them. Only about 5% of the population study personal development – our exact estimate of the percentage of professional performers in this country. Interesting, isn't it? The masses seem to view personal development as motivational nonsense. Of course, most of these people are struggling to make ends meet. In contrast, many world-class people, and those who aspire to world-class levels, are believers in the personal-development movement. You don't have to convince a champion to want to win. Personal development, by definition, is about discovering the unique talents, abilities and potentials that lie dormant within us. The great ones are always looking for that one little adjustment, strategy, distinction or technique that will give them an edge over the competition, and that's exactly what personal development offers. As Bill Gove was famous for saying, "All of us already have everything we need inside of us to make our lives work. Personal development is not about self-improvement . . . it's about self-discovery. It's about rediscovering what we already know."

▶ **ACTION STEP FOR TODAY**

Make a commitment to attend two seminars and/or workshops in the next twelve months for your own personal growth and development. Set a goal to listen to one of your favorite non-fiction authors/speakers every day when you're in the car. Set another goal to read one positive/inspirational book a month for the next twelve months. Map out a personal development plan of action and you'll be amazed at the results.

102
The Great Ones Are Problem Solvers

"We teach collaborative problem-solving.
In school, it's called cheating."
— Edward Bales, director of education, Motorola

The goal of world-class performers is to solve problems fast and move on to solving bigger, more complex problems. After all, the great ones know business and enterprise are based on problem solving. It's the cornerstone of commerce. Amateurs tend to spend more time jockeying for position to gain favor from their superiors than they do solving problems. Amateurs are looking for instant ego gratification and need to be given proper credit and recognition for their problem-solving prowess. Champions are more team-oriented. They know they are simply a cog in the wheel of a mastermind machine, where the sum of the group intelligence and experience dwarfs individual ability. The great ones are not interested in management kudos; they are interested in results. Professional performers' teams solve the problem and plead with management for more responsibility, then solve the next set of problems and beg management for even greater responsibility. Champions repeat this cycle over and over until they land the position they envision. This is one of the reasons the great ones write their own ticket in corporate America. While average people are complaining about being overworked and underpaid, pros know their ticket to the executive suite is paved with problem solving. When champions want a raise, they don't have to ask for one. All they have to do is help the organization solve larger, more complex problems, and increased compensation will follow. The world class understands increased compensation is the effect; problem solving and adding value is the cause. Instead of wishing and begging for more money, the great ones attack the cause, and the effect eventually takes care of itself.

▶ ACTION STEP FOR TODAY

Ask this critical thinking question: "Am I willing to solve larger, more complex problems in exchange for increased compensation?" If the answer is yes, go to your boss today and ask for more responsibility. There is never a lack of money in any organization for a person who can solve major problems. The next time you are daydreaming about making more money, stop daydreaming and ask for a bigger problem to solve.

▶▶ WORLD-CLASS RESOURCE

If you're in commission sales, get a copy of Bob Proctor's classic CD album, Your Mission in Commission. This is the best resource I've ever studied on commission sales. Bob Proctor tells it like it is, without the fluff. This is real-world material, delivered by one the great masters of commission sales. You can purchase this program at www.bobproctor.com

103

Champions Are Obsessed With Productivity And Results

"We know where most of the creativity, the innovation, the stuff that drives productivity lies – in the minds of those closest to the work. It's been there, in front of our noses, all along while we've been running around chasing robots and reading books on how to become Japanese –- or at least manage like them."

– Jack Welch, chairman and CEO, General Electric

Average performers think of work in terms of time invested on the job. World-class performers think of work in terms of overall productivity, output and results. Middle-class performers are far more concerned with what's for lunch than with the productivity of the business day. Their bodies are at work, but their minds are elsewhere. Professional performers tend to work in jobs and businesses they love. As a result, thoughts of how to be more successful and productive rarely leave their mind. The great ones have to force themselves into nonwork activities just to give their mind a chance to rest and recover. Is it any wonder why the world class controls over 90% of the wealth in America? The only people pros are competing against are other pros – about 5% of the workforce. The amateurs are no match for pros. How could they be? How can a person who is half engaged honestly expect to go head to head with the great ones? They can't, and they don't, which is why middle-class performers will always live middle-class existences. Don't misunderstand: they have the intelligence, talent, and ability to go pro, but they usually lack the will. Meanwhile, the great ones are the most sought-after group of business leaders in the world. They are welcome in any organization during good times and bad. The world class has an open ticket anywhere they want to go because they are obsessed with increasing productivity and achieving results.

▶ ACTION STEP FOR TODAY

Rate your professional productivity on a scale of 1 to 7, 7 being highest. If you scored less than a 6, make a list of three things you could do to increase your overall productivity. After you make your list, go to your boss and ask for additional suggestions. This one exercise may double or even triple your productivity and results.

104

The World Class Is Profit Driven

"Profitability is a necessary condition for existence and a means to more important ends, but it is not the end in itself for many of the visionary companies. Profit is like oxygen, food, water, and blood for the body; they are not the point of life, but without them, there is no life."

– *James Collins and Jerry Porras, authors of Built to Last*

The masses seem to have a collective belief that profit equates to greed. Professional performers understand that profit is what keeps the doors open, and what supports the ongoing innovation a company needs to compete. While the world class knows profit is the lifeblood of business, they are also aware of the power and responsibility that go with it. Give amateur performers a profit surplus, and greed kicks in. Do the same with pros, and watch as they turn their sights to a higher level of consciousness. They consider how they can reinvest and disperse extra money beyond the normal profit margin into their community and the world at large. The great ones tend to view the world as one big community that's increasingly interdependent. They seem to follow the "To whom much is given, much is expected" philosophy. Pros are aware that profit may not be the purpose of a business, but without it, there is no business. On a larger scale, without profit there is no financial contribution to send back to a world in need. The world class operates on a global level of awareness, and the amateurs should be glad they do. While middle-class thinkers are worrying about who's going to win the Super Bowl or the World Series, the great ones are working to do their part as leaders to ensure the world is better off tomorrow than it is today.

▶ **ACTION STEP FOR TODAY**

Reinvest a small amount of your profit or extra money back into your community. It's not the amount that's important; it's the habit. See how it makes you feel to circulate your abundance.

105

The Great Ones Take Responsibility

"Success on any major scale requires you to accept responsibility . . . In the final analysis, the one quality that all successful people have…is the ability to take on responsibility."
– *Michael Korda, author*

One of the critical factors separating amateurs from pros is responsibility. People operating at the poverty- and working-class levels of awareness often see themselves as victims of the powerful. They create invisible mental barriers that, in their minds, hold them back from moving up. They blame other people for keeping them down, such as their parents, friends and others of influence during their childhood. People at the middle-class level of awareness are a little more evolved, but tend to make safety and security their number one priorities. They hold on so tightly to what they have that they fail to see the real abundance staring them straight in the face. Average people in this category are terrified of losing what they have, because their mind is submerged in the cesspool of scarcity. People at this level truly believe their supply of money is limited, and if they lose what they have, they will never get it back. The majority of the population has this belief. People operating at the upper-class level of awareness tend to be unafraid, aggressive, ultra-competitive warriors who approach life like a battle. They know there is abundance and they are out to get it. The upper class tends to operate primarily from their ego. People at the world-class level are a step ahead of the upper class, simply because they operate from their spirit-self rather than their ego-self. The great ones have a thought process, philosophy and habit all rolled into one that overshadows the rest: I am responsible. The world class realizes they are completely responsible for their success or failure, as well as responsible for giving back some of the blessings bestowed upon them as a result of their tremendous success. Operating from a world-class level of awareness almost always precedes their success. The great ones keep marching forward, making a difference in themselves and the world.

▶ **ACTION STEP FOR TODAY**

Commit to taking total responsibility for everything that happens to you. This one change in thinking has the power to launch you to the world-class level faster than any other single idea.

106

Champions Take Risks

> "I don't want to find myself in a nursing home someday, thinking that all I did was play it safe."
> – *Charlie Eitel, Chairman/CEO, The Simmons Company*

Average performers are risk averse. They've been taught that to make it through life in one piece, play it safe and be thankful they have a roof over their head. "Stay below the radar and you won't get hurt," seems to be their world view. With a mindset rooted in fear and scarcity, they unconsciously set a goal of arriving safely at death. World-class performers work from an abundance-based consciousness rooted in love, which knows no limits or bounds. The pros take risks – not because they are necessarily more courageous – but because they believe they can get back anything they lose. In the minds of champions, resources and money are abundant. As a result, the fear of loss has very little influence with this group. Champions have always been risk takers, because they have come to understand that business and life are about learning and growing. How can you learn and grow when you never step out and try something new and exciting? There is never a lack of resources, only a lack of ideas. Without risk, there can be no progress. All of us only have so much sand left in the hourglass, and one day our sand will run out. The time to risk is now and the great ones know it.

▶ ACTION STEP FOR TODAY

Learning to be comfortable when taking calculated risks is an acquired skill. The only way to develop it is to begin to take risks. Decide today to take a small risk on something you've been thinking about doing. Feel the fear, and do it anyway. If this process is new to you, rest assured – you will feel less fear with every risk you take.

107

The World Class Has Tremendous Self-Respect

"A flippant, frivolous man may ridicule others, may controvert them, scorn them; but he who has any respect for himself seems to have renounced the right of thinking meanly of others."

– Johann Wolfgang von Goethe, 1749-1832, German dramatist

The poverty-, working- and middle-class levels of consciousness tend to struggle with respect. Respecting others is directly related to respecting yourself. It's been said "You cannot give what you do not have," and respect falls directly into this category. Respecting other people is easier for a pro because he has great respect for himself. The struggles and battles he has waged forged his confidence and character far beyond that of the average person. It's difficult for an intelligent person to play it safe every day and walk away with solid self-respect. It might be easier for the amateur if he was less talented or less intelligent than the pro. Yet they are not. In some cases, an amateur can be even more gifted than the pro. But the amateur has settled for a life of mediocrity, and deep down, they know it. They are dying with their music still inside. This often causes great sadness and even depression. To know you are capable of world-class performance and decide to play it safe is a hard concept to stomach for an able-minded individual. Sometimes the television, the ball game, the movies, or the alcohol are enough to drown out that little voice whispering that life is passing them by, and sometimes it is not. As a result, low self-esteem and self-respect tend to breed low respect for others. This thought process has done a lot of harm throughout the world. Human beings are emotional creatures who crave respect. When they don't get it, they begin to cause trouble. The world-class performer, on the other hand, is fully engaged in life and living. His self-respect lends itself to respect others. When he is not respected by others, he chalks it up to middle-class mentality. After all, he thinks to himself, aren't amateurs supposed to act like amateurs?

▶ **ACTION STEP FOR TODAY**

Ask this critical thinking question: "What single habit, action or behavior could I upgrade or change that would increase my level of self-respect?" Next, make a commitment, in writing, to make this upgrade or change in the next thirty days. Do the same thing every month for the next twelve months, and watch your life transform.

108

Champions Know Revenge Is For Amateurs

"The middle class broods and vows revenge when they feel cheated. The upper class attacks their abusers, intent on inflicting pain. The world class forgives their enemies and sends them love, because the emotional pro knows that the emotional amateur knows not."

– Steve Siebold

Depending on whether they are operating primarily from spirit or ego, amateurs tend to be interested in the idea of revenge. Many amateurs believe their lack of success and fulfillment is someone else's fault, which leads to thoughts of getting even. Revenge as a strategy is not limited to the middle class. Many very successful upper-class performers still believe in striking back at their competitors. The upper class often owes their tremendous financial success to the drive that is stimulated by their large egos. Unfortunately, this ego-driven consciousness is often also responsible for their lack of personal fulfillment. The upper class tends to believe the key to fulfillment is to gain greater success, and they are baffled when this formula doesn't work. The upper class is operating out of fear, and this mindset says revenge on the so-called guilty party will give them satisfaction. Of course, it doesn't. Amateurs also look for ego gratification in revenge. Their ego has been hurt, and they believe hitting back will repair the damage and allow them to save face. The cycle keeps repeating itself and delivers nothing but misery. The world class, operating out of love and abundance, dismisses revenge as a strategy for people operating at lower-level awareness. The great ones know you can't fight hate with hate. The only power in the universe worth projecting is the power of love. The pros know if they are cheated by an amateur, it's to be expected, because amateurs act out of fear. Their fear-based consciousness thinks irrationally, so their improper or unethical acts are to be expected. Champions feel empathy for amateurs, because all of the great ones are former amateurs themselves.

▶ ACTION STEP FOR TODAY

Decide today to abandon any thoughts or plans of revenge. Don't confuse forgiveness with weakness; anyone can hold a grudge. It takes a person operating at a higher level of awareness to forgive. Be reminded that 95% of the population is operating out of a consciousness of fear and scarcity, which is probably the reason this individual cheated you.

109

Champions Keep Things In Perspective

"In most situations, we don't need to slow down, we need to calm down."

– Bob Proctor, author, speaker

Amateur performers often crack under pressure because they lose their perspective. Their fear of losing overwhelms them to the point of physical, emotional and spiritual breakdown. The champion knows that the secret to performing well under pressure has more to do with their perception of the event than the event itself. While the amateur is telling himself that he must win, the pro is reminding herself that it's only a game. Both performers want to win, but the pro always outperforms the amateur under pressure because she has learned how to calm her nerves by putting things in perspective. Some people claim that champions perform better than any other group under pressure. This is not true. There is an inverse relationship between pressure and performance, no matter who you are or what you do. As pressure increases, performance decreases. This occurs whether you're Donald Trump or Donald Duck. The reason champions get better results is because they have trained themselves how to perceive the so-called pressure situation. The amateur perceives it as a threat, which triggers a fight or flight response from the mind and body. Physiologically speaking, the performer believes he is literally fighting for his life. Meanwhile, the pro has convinced herself that this situation is just a game, and that nobody dies from losing a game. This championship self-talk can be learned and implemented by anyone, but is rarely picked up on by amateurs. The world class has learned that developing and maintaining a crystal-clear perspective on the relative significance of their performance lives is critical to their success.

▶ **ACTION STEP FOR TODAY**

List the three events that cause you the most stress on a regular basis. Now ask this critical thinking question: "What would I need to say to myself on a daily basis to put these events in proper perspective to reduce or eliminate the stress they have caused me in the past?"

▶▶▍ **WORLD-CLASS RESOURCE**

Read Don't Sweat the Small Stuff, by Richard Carlson. This book will inspire you to believe that "It's all small stuff!"

110

The World Class Raises Their Rate Of Vibration At Will

"Ladies, do you want to know how to take a one-carat diamond and turn it into a two-and-a-half-carat diamond? Learn how to raise your ROV."

– Polly Bauer, former president/CEO of Home Shopping Network Credit Corporation

The average performer spends little time analyzing her own performance. Once she reaches a level of competence that satisfies her job requirements, ongoing analysis and improvement are no longer a priority. The world class is constantly analyzing, critiquing, and giving themselves feedback. One of the things a professional performer pays close attention to is her level of attraction to other people, especially prospects and customers. At Mental Toughness University, we call it Rate of Vibration, or ROV. The concept of ROV is simple: it's a combination of the mental and physical energy being projected from one person to another. You might call it charisma in action. The five components of ROV are energy, enthusiasm, confidence, belief and clarity. The sum total of these components is your ROV. At Mental Toughness University, we ask our sales and management clients to track their ROV on a scale of one to one thousand before and after every sales call or coaching session. The purpose is to convince the performer a high ROV creates greater attraction and response from the prospect or customer. Then, we show them how to raise their ROV in seconds. Professional performers have been using this concept for years. (It falls under various names.) The bottom line: the pro always contemplates what she thinks about in performance situations, and implementing strategies and techniques such as ROV creates better results. No matter where she is in her career, a champion is borderline obsessed with improving. She continues to learn new ideas and ways of improving her performance. Meanwhile, the middle-class performer is still doing things the way she was twenty years ago. The difference is more about consciousness than anything else.

▶ ACTION STEP FOR TODAY

Develop the habit of tracking your ROV during presentations and other times you are attempting to persuade people to your point of view. On a scale of 1 to 1,000, the average salesperson scores around 250. Top salespeople score around 750. The goal is to get as close to the 1,000 mark as possible. All scores are subjective, but the purpose of the exercise is to recognize the impact raising your ROV has on your ability to influence and persuade other people.

ENERGY - *Mental, Physical, Spiritual*

+

ENTHUSIASM - *Product, Customer, Self*

+

CONFIDENCE - *Product, Self, Customer, Company*

+

BELIEF - *Self, Product, Results*

+

CLARITY - *Vision, Purpose, Payoff (Significance)*

= R.O.V
RATE OF VIBRATION

1 -1,000 Scale

Average Performer's R.O.V. = 250

Top 1% of Performer's R.O.V. = 750

Your R.O.V. = _____

▶▶❙ WORLD-CLASS RESOURCE

Read The Power of Your Subconscious Mind, by Joseph Murphy, Ph.D.

111

The Pros Reward Themselves For Execution

"The goals, targets and rewards system is the wave of the future. Goals are execution-based; targets are results-based; and rewards are based on the successful completion of the goals, not the targets. This subtle shift in performance philosophy has the power to launch a performer from middle-class to world-class results."

– Steve Siebold

The masses tend to ignore the concept of creating a reward system to compliment their goal setting – those who actually set goals, that is. Professional performers use rewards to create ongoing motivation for themselves and others. Amateurs use rewards for themselves and their subordinates for achieving results. Sounds like a good concept, doesn't it? While it's not a bad idea, champions have a much better system. Champions set execution-based goals over which they have total control. The results they are aiming for, but don't have complete control over, are known as Targets. The great ones aim for their Targets but focus on their goals. For example, salespeople set a goal to make a certain number of calls. If they fail to make that number of calls, they fail to reach the goal. They are reprimanded and possibly penalized. If they accomplish the number of calls, they automatically earn the reward, no matter the outcome of those calls. That's execution-based goal setting. The philosophy is simple: reward people for doing what they say they are going to do, based on activities they can control. To reward someone for increasing sales, market share, or any outcome-based goal is a reward for something they only played a part in achieving, and they are being penalized under the same criteria. It only makes partial sense, and it can destroy the motivation of the performer. Rewarding execution-based performance is the wave of the future, because it's a much more accurate award, actually deserved. The priority is still set on bottom-line results, but the focus is toward high-quality, consistent execution. Reward performers for keeping their word and you build a success cycle of confidence and enthusiasm.

▶ **ACTION STEP FOR TODAY**

Take your number one goal for the next ninety days and convert it to a target. Next, make a list of every activity you must complete to attain your target. Lastly, think of a reward for yourself upon successful completion of the goal. I would strongly suggest converting all your current goals to targets over the next thirty days. After you get in the habit of this innovative approach, you'll be amazed at how much more motivated you will be to succeed.

112

Great Leaders Understand Recognition

"I have discovered a fascinating thing: men will die for ribbons."
– Napoleon, 1769-1821, emperor of France

Average performers tend to believe money and material possessions are their greatest motivators, yet I haven't seen a single study that backs this up. Amateurs don't know themselves as well as they might think. The human mind is a complex computer with deep recesses that must be fully explored if we are to truly know ourselves and what drives us. The only way this can be achieved is through extensive introspection. This is one of the reasons some performers visit therapists and counselors when they are not really in need of serious attention. It gives them a sounding board, an opportunity to have someone listen and ask intelligent, probing, introspective questions no one has ever asked them before. Ask a counselor how many people visit each week for this reason – you might be surprised. World-class performers know themselves, and they know what drives them. The single most popular motivator for performers of all classes is recognition, even though many people won't admit it. Human beings are emotional creatures who may be embarrassed by the fact that they are not entirely logical. It's almost as though logic has more credibility . . . except with the world class. They will tell you they are highly motivated by recognition. Recognition is the master motivator because it validates us to ourselves, and reminds us that we really are good enough, smart enough and competent enough. Most people are walking around with an inferiority complex of one kind or another from years of negative programming from parents, teachers, coaches and other amateurs of great influence. This programming can be overcome, but recognition will always be a mental massage for a bruised psyche. Champions know and embrace this with themselves and their charges, while the amateurs struggle to become more logical.

▶ ACTION STEP FOR TODAY

Set a goal to recognize the important people in your life for the things they do. Words of recognition are long remembered and highly treasured. Developing this habit may do more to solidify and grow your key relationships than anything else.

▶▶I WORLD-CLASS RESOURCE

If you manage or employ people, get a copy of 1001 Ways to Reward Employees, by Bob Nelson. This creative book is loaded with ideas on how to recognize and reward people for superior performance.

113

Champions Know The Power Of Programming

"The programming that you accept from others, and the conscious and unconscious directives, pictures, feelings and thoughts that you transmit to yourself, will find a place in your own internal control center. Together, those thoughts and images will continue to create in advance, or influence on the spot, every response, attitude, and action that will be a part of you and your future."

– *Dr. Shad Helmstetter, author*

The majority of champions I've worked with and coached during the years confess the bulk of the mental programming they received during their childhoods was substandard. Many are quick to add that the people who programmed them – parents, teachers, coaches, ministers and adults of influence – were doing the best they could, based on their level of awareness at the time. It's easy to criticize in hindsight, yet champions don't feel the need to do this. They want to take control of their own reprogramming process and install the habits, philosophies, traits and beliefs that empower, rather than limit them. Middle-class performers scoff at things like reprogramming and tend to hold on to what they were taught, no matter how poor their teachers' thinking. The pros use two primary methods of reprogramming. First and foremost, they alter the language they use when they talk to themselves and others. They adjust their language from the middle-class to the world-class level. They create self-talk scripts and repeat them daily until the change takes place. The second thing they do is use the power of mental pictures, or visualization training, to adjust how they experience events. The combination of these two change processes has a powerful effect on the mindset of the performer. Sadly, the concepts are so simple that most people miss them. Meanwhile, the great ones keep getting stronger and stronger by developing world-class thoughts, feelings and attitudes through the reprogramming process.

▶ ACTION STEP FOR TODAY

Make the decision today to take responsibility for old programming that does not serve you. Practice reprogramming your old programs by altering your language and using visualization training.

▶▶I WORLD-CLASS RESOURCE

Pick up a copy of The Self-Talk Solution, by Dr. Shad Helmstetter. This book contains more than 2,500 self-talk programming messages of the world class. Dr. Helmstetter is the genius of the self-talk revolution. I've been studying his work since 1986, and it's changed my life immeasurably.

114

Champions Are Of Good Cheer

"If you want to live a long, healthy, and prosperous life, make a commitment to yourself to always be of good cheer.

It will affect everything and everyone around you."
– Bill Gove, 1912-2001, the father of professional speaking

Amateurs inadvertently create their own mediocrity by the thoughts they entertain. Professional performers consciously create world-class results by carefully constructing every thought. The foundation of this philosophy seems to begin with a sunny disposition. In other words, the world class is of good cheer by conscious choice. The great ones are acutely aware their thoughts create their circumstances, while the masses continue to reverse the equation. Is the world class so happy because their lives are so fulfilling; or are their lives so fulfilling because they are happy? Champions know that their inner world determines their outer world. Knowing this, they act the part of the successful, fulfilled and happy person until the part becomes them. They have learned that, in order to attract extraordinary success, fulfillment and happiness, they must first become these things. The great ones have a saying about this: "Whatever you are looking for is looking for you." It's a well-known law of the universe that like attracts like, success breeds success, and happiness manifests happiness. While the middle class waits to win the lottery, graduate from school, get a job, or any number of things before they decide to be happy, they attract feelings of longing and lack. This doesn't occur by accident. We don't attract what we want; we attract what we are. This is why the world class chooses to be of good cheer.

▶ ACTION STEP FOR TODAY

Make the decision every morning to have a sunny disposition. Watch carefully and study how many others you attract with the same good cheer.

▶▶ı WORLD-CLASS RESOURCE

Get An Attitude of Gratitude: 21 Life Lessons, by Keith Harrell. When it comes to being of good cheer, Keith Harrell is the master. I own every book, tape and CD album he's ever produced. No wonder he is called "Dr. Attitude."

115

The Great Ones Are Learning Machines

"An organization's ability to learn, and translate that learning into action rapidly, is the ultimate competitive business advantage."

– Jack Welch, former chairman and CEO, General Electric

For most people in modern western culture, learning means memorizing facts, theories, theorems and dates. That's what most of us were taught to do in school. To average people, learning is a late-night cram session and a pot of coffee to stay awake. Professional performers have overcome this outdated, industrial-age system and created a formula for learning and developing their minds. As speaker Jim Rohn says, "Formal education will make you a living; self-education will make you a fortune." The pros know this to be accurate, and invest heavily in books, tapes, and CD programs on everything from personal development to business sales, marketing and management. They read and study trade journals and become world-renowned experts. Average people spend less than ten dollars annually on books. The top 1% of income earners in America invest nearly $10,000 annually on books and other learning resources. They attend seminars, workshops and retreats. Amateur performers look at these investments as a waste of time and money. They are more likely to invest their money in lottery tickets, satellite television, cigarettes, alcohol, and other forms of entertainment. The great ones, in the words of scientific genius Buckminster Fuller, "Dare to be naïve." The middle class thinks they have little left to learn. World-class performers know the more they learn, the greater the level of awareness they reach; and the greater the level of awareness, the more they realize how much more there is left to learn. The great ones know learning, like love, is infinite. There is no end until their hearts stop beating.

▶ **ACTION STEP FOR TODAY**

Make a commitment to develop your own self-education program. Read, listen, and attend seminars and workshops. Set a goal to read a certain number of books and listen to a set number of CDs each month. This shift in lifestyle will catapult your career and your consciousness.

▶▶I **WORLD-CLASS RESOURCE**

Invest in a copy of Lead the Field, by Earl Nightingale. This album was recorded in 1960, and its message is timeless. It's a 6-cassette/CD album that deserves a place in your personal library. You can find out more about it at www.nightingale.com

116

Champions Change Their Emotional Responses

"It's not the event itself that does us in, it's how we perceive it."
– Dr. Karl Menninger, psychiatrist, author

One of the most powerful tools used by world-class performers is called the Ten-Step Change Process. It helps alter the way they respond to events outside their control. For example, a salesperson makes a presentation to a customer who treats the salesperson poorly and disrespectfully. The emotional response of amateurs would be anger. The pro realizes treating people disrespectfully is classic amateur behavior. Through the Ten-Step Change Process, the performer writes down the activating event (the disrespectful customer). Next, he writes down his response. Then he decides if that response is helping or hurting. The next step is to decide whether his response was rational or irrational. Next, he examines his thought process thoroughly, and identifies his ultimate response if this were to happen again. He then mentally rehearses implementing the new response. Next, he creates a written script of the new response, and rehearses the new response twice a day, visually and verbally. He examines his response the next time the event occurs. If he is satisfied with the result, he has successfully transformed his response to this event. If he's not yet satisfied, he continues the process until the desired behavior change takes place. This is one of the most effective change processes of the world class. Knowing it is worthless unless you use it. Are you ready to go pro yet? Imagine the potential if you could alter every major response that you encountered on a daily basis. Would that elevate you to the next level?

▶ ACTION STEP FOR TODAY

Select one event that triggers a negative emotional response and put it through the Ten-Step Change Process. For example, do you get angry when someone cuts you off in traffic, or when people treat you disrespectfully, or when your son or daughter gets a poor grade on a report card? Our habitual responses are based on our perceptions of what these events mean and our perceptions can be altered or even totally changed in a very short period of time through reprogramming. Give yourself twenty-one to thirty days to make the transformation.

THE 10 STEPS TO POSITIVE CHANGE

You respond to your perception of an event. *Client treats me like dirt, ignores me and makes me feel insignificant. It makes me angry and I want to tell him off. Who does he think he is? I feel frustrated and mad.*

Decide if your response is helping or hurting you. *It's hurting me because it puts me in a bad mood.*

Decide if your response is rational or irrational. *Rational - he acted like a jerk!*

Examine your response in detail through meta-cognition. (Think about what you think about) *I'm thinking to myself, "I'm only trying to do my job, he could at least be decent to me, after all, I'm a professional, too".*

Identify your ultimate response if this situation were to occur again. *Don't let it bother me, because he's just a fallible human being, just like me. He just doesn't have the people skills that I do. He's under pressure and he's taking it out on me. His response has nothing to do with me. All I need to focus on is my part of the equation - That's all I can control.*

Create a mental rehearsal of your ideal response. *I see myself responding calmly and quietly - and reminding myself that this person is an emotional amateur.*

Write a script that supports your ideal response. *I'm cool, calm and collected both inside and out, no matter what. I do this because its the best thing I can do for me.*

Rehearse your ideal visual and verbal responses twice a day. *Rehearse mentally and verbally before I walk into the prospect's office.*

Examine your response the next time this or a similar event occurs.

If you are satisfied with your new perception/response, you have successfully constructed a new neural pathway and created a positive change in your life. If you're not satisfied, continue visualizing and verbalizing your new perception/response and test until positive change occurs.

▶▶I WORLD-CLASS RESOURCE

For further study of creating change through emotional control, visit www.rebt.org This website belongs to Dr. Albert Ellis, who pioneered Rational-Emotive Behavior Therapy. The site offers free information as well as additional resources on related topics.

117

The Great Ones Have A Sense Of Urgency

"One realizes the full importance of time only when there is little of it left. Every man's greatest capital asset is his unexpired years of productive life."
– P.W. Litchfield

Middle-class performers operate like there is an endless amount of time in a day, week, month, year and life. The world class is extremely sensitive to time. The great ones have a sense of urgency because they are operating at a level of awareness that constantly reminds them the present moment is all any of us really have. The world class is on a mission to fulfill a dream, and they know the clock is ticking. The only time amateur performers develop a sense of urgency is toward the end of the day, week, or before they go on vacation. Imagine if they channeled that same energy, enthusiasm and focus into their everyday performance. Worldwide productivity would probably triple in one day. Professional performers constantly remind themselves that life is short and if they are going to make something happen, now is the time. This thought process makes the middle class uncomfortable. Remember, they prefer to operate in a state of mild delusion. Knowing the clock is ticking and none of us know how much time we have left is too uncomfortable for emotional amateurs. For pros, who operate from objective reality, it's a primary motivating force. It's one of the reasons the great ones tend to pursue large, magnificent visions. They know their time on earth is limited and they want to leave a legacy. Their sense of urgency goes back to the beginning of the mental toughness process – clearly defining what you want. What do you have a sense of urgency to do? If you know the answer, you can implement this world-class philosophy immediately. If not, make it your mission to discover the embers that burn within your soul and focus that passion on what you really want. Don't stop until you find it. When you do, create a sense of urgency to act on it now. Don't hesitate. Pursue your dream boldly and fearlessly. It may be later than you think.

▶ ACTION STEP FOR TODAY

To heighten your sense of urgency, do a little mathematical calculation. Based on statistics, the average man living in 21st century America will live seventy-three years. The average woman will live seventy-nine years. Based on your current age and these statistics, how many days do you have left to live? Keep this number in front of you as a reminder the clock is ticking and there is no time to lose.

HOW MANY DAYS DO YOU HAVE LEFT IF YOU LIVE THE AVERAGE LIFE SPAN?

The Average Man Lives 73 Years

The Average Woman Lives 79 Years

Source: Dept of Health and Human Services

118

The World Class Believes In Servant Leadership

"The measure of a man is . . . in the number
of people who he serves."

– Paul D. Moody

The world class sees themselves as servants in their personal and professional lives. Whatever their chosen field, the great ones know the essence of success and fulfillment can be found in the service of others. Professional performers understand that amateurs suffer the consequences of living out of a fear-based consciousness. Most pros are recovering amateurs who woke up one day and made a decision to change. They empathize with the amateur mindset and do everything they can to lead them to the next level of consciousness. Champions believe the greatest leaders are the greatest servants, and that all of us are here to lend a hand to one another. In order to embrace this mindset and become a conduit for positive change, a person must be operating from spirit, as opposed to ego. Champions serve without asking or expecting anything in return. Of course, in accordance with the law of cause and effect, they are richly rewarded for their efforts. The middle-class consciousness is not operating at a level high enough to see this law in action. When we were kids, most of us learned the saying, "The more you give, the more you get." Somewhere along the way, many of us have forgotten this piece of ancient wisdom. As a result, amateurs are always seeing how much they can get without having to give. On the other hand, the world class continues to give out of love and activate this law. The law is the same for everyone, yet amateurs don't believe in it. They are afraid they will serve someone without getting anything in return, and they are afraid they'll get hurt again. Fear draws them inside themselves and reinforces their amateur behavior. Meanwhile, the world class is humbly serving society and being handsomely rewarded.

▶ **ACTION STEP FOR TODAY**

Examine your beliefs about serving others, and ask this critical thinking question: "What do my habits, actions and behaviors say about my belief in the law of cause and effect?" On a scale of 1 to 7, 7 being the highest, how much do you really give to others?

119

The Great Ones Make The Complicated Simple

"Genius is the ability to reduce the complicated to the simple."
– C. W. Ceram, Roman archeologist, author

The middle-class consciousness seems to have a belief that the more complicated something sounds, the more impressive it is. The world class tends to have the opposite belief. They know even the most complex ideas, philosophies, or systems can be broken down into simple concepts. Albert Einstein's theory of relativity is one of the greatest discoveries of the 20th century, and even scientists agree the formula is complex. Einstein disagreed. Explaining the basic theory to a non-scientist one day, he said; "Have you ever spent time with a pretty girl and the time just flew by? Have you ever spent time with someone you didn't like and the time seemed to drag on forever? That's relativity." The great ones know true genius rests in the simplification of what appear to be complex processes. Amateurs are convinced success has to be more than the simple implementation of a few dozen key ideas, habits, thought processes and philosophies. Amateurs make the success process more complex than it is. Large corporations are made up of a series of complex systems, but every great business leader will tell you 90% of all business problems can be solved by increased sales. Champions constantly try to simplify their thoughts and ideas. Mental clarity is the cornerstone of everything they do, and simplifying things promotes greater clarity.

▶ **ACTION STEP FOR TODAY**

Do a breakdown to discover the essence of what motivates, inspires and drives you, and most importantly, what makes you happy. Reduce these ideas to as few words as possible, so a fourth grader could understand what you're saying. This exercise will elevate your level of mental clarity.

120

Champions Understand Success

"If a man has done his best, what else is there?"
– Gen. George S. Patton, 1885-1945, U.S. Army

Success, to average performers, means money and material possessions. To champions, these are outward manifestations of success, but not success itself. The pros know success is a simple concept. Champions tend to believe success is giving your family, work and life your very best effort, and that's it. End of definition. After all, the champions say, what else is there? No idea has been so maligned and manipulated as success. Amateurs will have you believe success is what Madison Avenue tells us it is through slick advertising campaigns. The great advertisers know people hunger for success, and they represent it as owning the right home, car, clothes, etc. They have obviously studied their customer, and are being richly rewarded for their service. The world class doesn't buy into psychographic advertising or anything else the profiteers say represents success. The great ones simply select their chosen field, write out their plan, create their vision, and go to work making it a reality. The simple day-by-day progression toward their vision spells success. When their outcome is achieved, they celebrate, all the while knowing their real measure of success was in doing, not having. The world class understands that to have, you must do, and to do, you must be. They focus on becoming the person they wish to become, and everything else falls into place.

▶ ACTION STEP FOR TODAY

Take inventory of your beliefs surrounding success. What does success really mean to you? Have you adopted the amateur or the professional definition of success? How are these beliefs impacting your everyday life and happiness?

121

Champions Thrive On World Class Self-Talk

"Repeat anything long enough and it will start to become you."
— Tom Hopkins, author, speaker

Self-talk is what we say to ourselves all day long, yet it's also how we say it. For years, philosophers, psychologists and performance experts worldwide have known about the impact self-talk has on us. That being said, average performers are oblivious to what they are saying to themselves and how it's affecting the quality of their lives. The pros have always been aware of the power of language in programming and reprogramming the human computer. Dr. Shad Helmstetter, in his magnificent book, What to Say When You Talk to Yourself, writes that up to 77% of the average person's self-talk is negative. According to Dr. Helmstetter, we spend our lives talking ourselves into and out of things. Champions believe and embrace this idea. As a matter of fact, the easiest way to know you're in the presence of champions is to listen to them. The world class has spent years overcoming poor programming, and this process usually begins with the use of language, both with themselves and others. The great ones believe almost anything is possible, simply because they have repeated that idea – and others like it – to themselves for years. To quote Dr. Helmstetter, "Repetition is a convincing argument." Developing world-class self-talk may be the most powerful of all of the mental toughness secrets of the great ones. Like most of the habits, traits and philosophies in this book, it's so simple that it's often overlooked. As a result, amateur performers continue to perpetuate amateur language with themselves and others. Meanwhile, the great ones create ideas out of thin air, convince themselves achievement is possible, and then go out and make it happen.

▶ ACTION STEP FOR TODAY

Begin monitoring everything you say to yourself and others. Ask this critical thinking question: "Is the way I use the language programming me for success or failure?" Next, begin listening to the way people around you use the language. Ask yourself the same question about them. This is an eye-opening experience.

▶▶ WORLD-CLASS RESOURCE

Visit www.milliondollarmind.com and invest in this Self -Talk CD album. I listen to them every morning as I'm getting ready for work, and all day long in the background in my office.

122

The Great Ones Know Salespeople Drive All Business

"We are all salespeople, every day of our lives. We are selling our ideas, our plans, our enthusiasms to those with whom we come in contact."

– Charles Schwab, former, CEO Bethlehem Steel

America boasts more than fifteen million salespeople, yet the image of salespeople among the amateur community is weak. The masses tend to look down at salespeople as hucksters and smooth talkers. The championship community, on the other hand, embraces and admires salespeople. They see them as the driving force of the global economy. Salespeople are the athletes of the business world. They drive production, manufacturing, research and development, management and just about every other sector of our society. In reality, there are only two kinds of jobs: sales and sales support. The average salesperson is keeping thirty-three people employed, in some form or another, based on his production. What other profession even comes close? The world class knows we are all salespeople. All of us are trying to sell our ideas, ourselves and our passions to other people. Selling is the natural order of human existence, and mentally tough performers hold the highest respect for professional salespeople. Salespeople are in the line of fire daily, making things happen and keeping the economy rolling along. They don't get the public accolades of the doctor, accountant, lawyer or banker, except from the champions. There's a kinship between them that can be explained by one word: respect.

▶ **ACTION STEP FOR TODAY**

Take stock of your attitude toward salespeople and the sales profession in general, whether you're in sales or something else. In reality, we are all salespeople, and your beliefs surrounding this critical skill will determine how successful you will be.

▶▶I **WORLD-CLASS RESOURCE**

Read Changing the Game, The New Way To Sell, by Larry Wilson.

123

Champions Know Security Is A Perception

"When you know you're capable of dealing with whatever comes, you have the only security that the world has to offer."
— *Harry Browne, investment advisor, author*

The endless quest for security is the plague of the middle-class level of consciousness. Security is an illusion used to ease the late nights of worry and concern about the future. The world class knows there are only two facts in which you can be secure: all of us were born, and all of us will die. Everything that happens in between these two dates is up for grabs. These realities invoke terror in the hearts of amateurs, but are liberating to champions, because they are indisputable. It may not be comforting, but it's reality. One of the hallmarks of the great ones is their ability to deal in straightforward and simple truths. Give it to them just as it is, without any spin. This fulfills their need to work from a point of objective reality, so they can devise a solid plan of action based on fact. Average performers cringe at the thought of not having security, but instead of evolving to a higher level of conscious awareness, most choose to delude themselves into a false sense of security. It's no wonder amateurs are no match for pros — it's not even a level playing field. Champions are motivated by the idea that their security is in their ability to perform. The great ones live for challenge, and often they love the battle for the prize more than the prize itself. They love the battle because they expect to win, and their positive expectation continues to grow with each subsequent victory. The world class knows that, if any form of security exists in the universe, it is within their thoughts. They are willing to court doubt and darkness along the road to enlightenment. Extrinsic things like money will never make you feel secure unless you are secure on the inside; unless you believe you have the ability to deal with whatever happens between your birthday and your death day. If this world-class thought process exists, almost anything, from a teddy bear to a million dollars, will enhance your feeling of security. If you don't have it, a billion dollars won't make you feel secure. Security is simply a perception, and the great ones have always known it.

▶ ACTION STEP FOR TODAY

Rate yourself on a scale of 1 to 7, 7 being highest: How confident are you in your ability to successfully handle anything that happens in your life? If you scored less than a 6, begin to build your confidence by upgrading your self-talk in this area. Thirty days of telling yourself that you have the ability to handle anything life throws you will start you on the path to world-class feelings of security.

124

The World Class Believes In Self-Reliance

"Follow your own path, no matter what people say."
– Karl Marx, 1818-1883, founder of modern communism

The middle-class consciousness tends to rely on other people's actions, opinions and behaviors. The world class learns to rely on themselves. They develop supreme self-confidence and a penchant for action. The philosophy of the world class is to take full responsibility for their successes and failures. Average performers want to blame everyone for everything. The smoker who gets sick from smoking wants to sue the tobacco company for his illness. The fast-food junkie becomes obese from ingesting hundreds of cheeseburgers and pizzas and blames the restaurants that served her. The poverty-, working- and middle-class levels of consciousness often have a victim mentality. Professional performers take responsibility for their decisions and exercise self-reliance. Maybe most importantly, champions don't look to other people to make them happy. The great ones know happiness is not something you get, it's something you are. While champions enjoy the company of others, they are just as happy to be alone. Their core level of contentment begins with them.

▶ **ACTION STEP FOR TODAY**

Identify an area of your life in which you rely on someone else. Next, make a commitment to take full responsibility for the results or outcomes you experience in this area, regardless of whether you are directly responsible. Start with your finances. Who is responsible for your accumulation of wealth? Your accountant? Banker? Broker? Financial planner? You are ultimately responsible. If you adopt this philosophy in every major area of your life, you will never slip into the blame game again.

▶▶❙ **WORLD-CLASS RESOURCE**

Get a copy of Self-Reliance and Other Essays by Ralph Waldo Emerson. Emerson was clearly operating at an elevated level of consciousness when he wrote his essay on self-reliance. It's a masterpiece that deserves a place in your personal library.

125

The Great Ones Manufacture Their Own Self-Image

"Self-esteem – high or low – tends to be a generator of self-fulfilling prophecies."
– Dr. Nathaniel Branden, psychologist, author

It's been said that self-image is the reputation we have with ourselves. It's also been said that most of us suffer from some type of inferiority complex. The world class has overcome this problem by realizing everyone on the planet is inferior and superior to everyone in some way. They believe people have multiple intelligences, depending on their personality styles and experiences. The artist might not be the best mechanic. The mathematician might not possess highly evolved creative faculties. Champions believe the question is not "Are you smart?" but "How are you smart?" The difference in this interpretation of intelligence is monumental. The self-image of the great ones is the foundation of their success. Champions have major-league credibility with themselves. This self-confidence manifests itself in various forms critical in their ascension to the world-class level. It affects the way they approach business, life and other people. It determines the size and scope of the vision they create for their lives. Champions believe almost anything is within their reach, based on the power of their own self-image. The primary strategies the great ones use to develop a powerful self-image are self-talk and mental imagery. While amateurs are talking themselves out of attempting large goals and expansive visions, the pros are talking themselves into it. The difference doesn't have anything to do with intelligence; it is programming the champions create for themselves. The great ones manufacture their own self-image from scratch – and so do the middle class.

▶ ACTION STEP FOR TODAY

Ask this critical thinking question: "Do I have the self-image necessary to manifest my ultimate vision for my life?" If the answer is no, write down three world-class affirmations about your vision that will help you develop a world-class self-image.

▶▶I WORLD-CLASS RESOURCE

Get a copy of The Six Pillars of Self-Esteem, by Dr. Nathaniel Branden. Dr. Branden was the protégé of novelist and philosopher Ayn Rand, as well as a pioneer in the self-esteem movement. Six Pillars is his magnum opus. This book will inspire you to examine your thought processes in a whole new way.

126

Champions Are Bold And Daring Visionaries

"Vision . . . it reaches beyond the thing that is, into the conception of what can be. Imagination gives you the picture. Vision gives you the impulse to make the picture your own."
— Robert Collier, 1885-1950, author

One of the most important habits of the great ones is the creation, nurturing and ongoing psychological evolution of their life's vision. Generally speaking, the middle-class consciousness is more involved in assisting world-class performers in achieving their vision. Amateur performers are aware of what vision is, but don't believe in the concept or themselves enough to create and manifest their own visions. The middle-class consciousness needs the emotional support of other people to make their visions reality. This is where the world class breaks away from the pack. The world-class consciousness is so powerful it needs little, if any, outside support to maintain motivation and direction toward its vision. The great ones have the confidence and clarity to go it alone, if necessary. That said, professional performers are the first group to build mentor and support teams. The difference lies in their mental strength and laser-like focus on their purpose and mission in life. Vision, to amateurs, is a company's statement on the first page of its annual report. Vision, to pros, is a clearly written, ten- to twenty-page (on average) double-spaced document they see as their personal Declaration of Independence. It is the result of years of soul-searching and self-discovery. It's the reason they're doing everything they do. They read it every day and think about it all the time. All the great philosophers of the last two thousand years have agreed on at least one thing: we become what we think about. Champions know this, so they think about their vision all the time. This is the primary reason for the psychological separation between the good and the great. Good performers turn off their vision when it's quitting time. Great performers never stop thinking about it. As a result, when the good and the great go head to head, it's a mismatch from the start. The great ones create their vision, and then their vision creates them.

▶ ACTION STEP FOR TODAY

Make a commitment to create the ultimate vision for your life in the next thirty days. Use these eight life components as a guide: business/career; family/friends, money/finances, recreation/fun, health/diet/exercise, faith/spiritual, social/cultural, and personal development. You can write these visions as independent components, or include all of them in one long vision. Use as much detail as possible to define what you want to be, have and do in your life. The last step is the most important: write about why you want these things to manifest. Include as much emotion as possible. Describe the feelings you are trying to create through the achievement of your vision.

▶▶❘ WORLD-CLASS RESOURCE

Read Visioning: The Ten Steps To Designing the Life of Your Dreams, by Lucia Capacchione, Ph.D.

127

Champions Never Say Die

"Never die easy. Why run out of bounds and die easy? Make that linebacker pay. It carries into all facets of your life. It's okay to lose, to die, but don't die without trying, without giving it your best."

— *Walter Payton, 1954-1999, professional football player*

The middle class will persist until they become uncomfortable. The upper class will persist until it becomes painful. The world class never says die. Champions are comfortable being uncomfortable, because they have grown so accustomed to risk that feelings of vulnerability almost seem natural. Champions don't even begin to pay attention until they feel pain, which they expect to feel on a regular basis. Champion cyclist Lance Armstrong says racing doesn't even get interesting until it becomes what he calls a "suffer-fest." Even the upper class cannot compete with the world class because, while good performers have a deep desire to win, the great ones are committed to winning. The distinction between the two thought processes is substantial. Failure to manifest the vision is not an option; champions will do it or die trying. The mantra they love to espouse is, "Whatever it takes." The great ones are masters of self-denial, suffering and sacrifice. They do it all to live their vision. If you're going to go up against the great ones, you better pack a lunch — it's going to be a long afternoon.

▶ **ACTION STEP FOR TODAY**

Ask this critical thinking question: "How committed am I to achieving my ultimate vision?" Are you really willing to do whatever it takes? If so, know you are on the right track. If not, chances are you have settled for second best in your vision. It doesn't have sufficient emotional energy to motivate you through the tough times that will undoubtedly occur. If the latter is the case, do some soul searching and rewrite your vision. Odds are that you will need world-class emotional energy to bring your dream into reality.

▶▌ WORLD-CLASS RESOURCE

Go inside the mind of one of the great champions as he fights for his life in Never Die Easy, by Walter Payton with Don Yaeger. This is the autobiography of one of the National Football League's greatest running backs, written in the midst of his battle with cancer. This book is like a blueprint on the thought processes, habits and traits of champions. If you ever saw the man they called "Sweetness" on the gridiron, this book will leave an indelible impression on your heart.

128

Champions Define Winning As Personal Progress

"The most evolved among us understand that winning is an inside job. It's not about beating or besting someone else, but rather getting the best from ourselves. Winning is about being better tomorrow than you were today."

– Bill Gove, 1912-2001, the father of professional speaking

To average performers, winning usually means beating someone else. To the world class, winning usually means besting their previous performance. The upper class is more ego-driven and competitive than the world class. The great ones have evolved from an ego-driven consciousness to a spirit-driven consciousness, which transcends their need to be better than someone else. Champions know the real game is you against you, a paradox only the great ones fully comprehend. The world class has come to the stark realization that life is not a level playing field, which makes true competition an illusion. People seeking ego gratification perpetuate the illusion of true and fair competition. Professional performers are Zen-like in their approach to winning, and tend to focus on execution-based performance goals they can completely control. This keeps them in line with the reality that the only parts of winning they can control are their personal effort and attitude. The great ones know the most accurate indicators of winning are their ongoing growth and evolution as performers, and more importantly, as human beings.

▶ ACTION STEP FOR TODAY

Just for today, make a commitment to transcend your ego-based desire to be better than anyone else. Focus all of your competitive efforts inward and see how much better you can be today than you were yesterday. Monitor how this elevated level of consciousness makes you feel. You may decide to adopt this thought process as a habit, and eventually, a belief that transcends the need to beat anyone at anything.

▶▶I WORLD-CLASS RESOURCE

Read Permission to Win, by Ray Pelletier.

129

Champions Know Abundant Health Begins With Body Weight

"A significant step you can take on the road to world-
class success and fulfillment is to get your body weight
under control. The confidence you will gain as a result
will carry over into every other area of your life."

– *Steve Siebold*

Professional performers know the foundation of good health
is weight control. They know disease often begins when body
weight is disproportionate. Champions focus on diet and exercise
to manage their weight and overall health. They also know the
real secret to weight control is commitment and mental toughness.
The poverty, working, and middle classes tend to believe the right
diet is the key to weight loss and control. The great ones realize
the best diet in the world is worthless without decision and commitment. They also know they are in total control of what they
eat and how they exercise, and if they slip out of balance in this
area they are quick to get back on track. Taking control of weight
through conscious choice is a fast track to ascending to world-class
levels in other areas of your life. For those who wish to ascend to
greatness, this is great place to begin. The confidence and power
being thin and healthy will give you cannot be overestimated.

▶ **ACTION STEP FOR TODAY**

Give yourself a mental toughness reality check: Remove all
your clothes, stand in front of a full-length mirror, and write a
paragraph on what you see. Next, ask this critical thinking question: "What level of consciousness does my body reflect?" Is it:

poverty class, working class, middle class, upper class or world class?

▶▶I WORLD-CLASS RESOURCE

To learn more about mental toughness in the process of weight control, visit www.diefatbook.com

130

The World Class Seeks The Wisdom Of The Ages

"I find television very educational. Every time someone turns it on, I go in the other room and read a book."
– Groucho Marx, 1890-1977, comedian, actor

Average performers tend to believe as long as they have acquired the necessary knowledge to perform in their job, it's no longer important to continue the education/learning process. The great ones are the busiest people in the marketplace. They always search for the most effective and efficient methods of learning. One favorite is reading and studying positive quotation books. These books are jam-packed with wisdom from the most highly evolved thinkers and performers. While most amateurs probably consider positive quotations to be "cheesy," the pros are studying them like scientists and benefiting from the wisdom of the ages. These books contain pure gold, and the champions know it. Amazingly, you can find these works sitting on discount racks at every major bookstore in the world. Very few people buy them. The masses are so focused on finding happiness through pleasure that they miss the fact that happiness is a byproduct of wisdom and self-discovery. The answers are in these books, yet the masses ignore them. This mindset is a microcosm which illustrates why the rich get richer and the poor, poorer. Human beings cannot remain stagnant – we are either growing or dying. We are either getting better or getting worse. The pros use quotation books as a method of ensuring they are on the path of learning and growth.

▶ ACTION STEP FOR TODAY

Make a commitment today to read at least five positive quotations every day for the rest of this year. The wisdom in these quotes will motivate, inspire and enlighten you.

▶▶I WORLD-CLASS RESOURCE

My favorite quotation book is The Best of Success, by Wynn Davis. This hardcover classic contains more than three hundred pages of some of the greatest things ever said about successful living. It's a must for your personal library. For a weekly success quote via e-mail, visit www.mentaltoughnessblog.com and sign up for this free service.

131

World-Class Employees See Themselves As Self-Employed

"In a study done in New York some years ago, researchers found that people who ranked in the top three percent in every field had a special attitude that set them apart from average performers in their industries. It was this: they viewed themselves as self-employed throughout their careers, no matter who signed their paychecks. They saw themselves as responsible for their companies, exactly as if they owned the companies personally."

– Brian Tracy, author, speaker

Most people who are employed by a company believe they work for someone else. Professional performers know everyone works for themselves. From the line worker on the factory floor to the top brass of the executive team, everyone is self-employed. Employees operating at the middle-class level of awareness tend to see themselves as cogs in the wheel of the organizational hierarchy. World-class employees see themselves as professional performers who lease their services to the company which employs them. This little distinction makes a huge difference when it comes to results. Amateurs feel enslaved; pros feel empowered. Amateurs feel trapped; pros feel free. Everyone who works in a free-market economy has the choice of where and to whom they want to lease their services. The companies are also free to hire or reject any free agent who applies. All parties are free to choose. Champions know the most significant benefit of being a professional performer is that they can write their own ticket. Every organization on the planet is searching for world-class performers. Only 5% of the population is at this level, and a substantial percentage of those

5% are business owners not available for hire. The great ones are doing things with the mindset of being self-employed, regardless of who signs their paycheck.

▶ **ACTION STEP FOR TODAY**

Decide to adopt the mindset of self-employment. No matter what title you hold, you are now CEO and president of your own personal services corporation. Next, ask this critical thinking question: "Would I hire me?"

132

The Great Ones Aren't Afraid To Suffer

"What makes a great endurance athlete is the ability to absorb potential embarrassment, and to suffer without complaint. I was discovering that, if it was a matter of gritting my teeth, not caring how it looked, and outlasting everybody else, I won. It didn't seem to matter what the sport was – in a straight-ahead, long-distance race, I could beat anybody. If it was a suffer-fest, I was good at it."

– Lance Armstrong, cyclist, six-time Tour de France champion

The world class knows success always comes with a price tag. While the middle class wastes their time searching for short cuts, the great ones get in the game and endure the pain and suffering every champion must endure. There is no escape. The road to victory is paved with blood, sweat and tears. On their quest to go pro, champions are not surprised when pain and suffering tags along. They see it as part of the process. They understand, at the core of their being, that championship mentality is a result of hanging tough through adversity, and it cannot be gained any other way. The mentally tough get tough by fighting so many battles – some lost, some won – that they eventually become great warriors. The pain and suffering process is to mental toughness what carbon is to steel. The middle class often sees taking the easy way out as victory, but in reality, they are robbing themselves of the exposure and experience they need to become great. It's the greatest tragedy of the middle class. They are so close to a life of success and fulfillment, yet so far away due to their own self-deception and unwillingness to meet life head on and endure the necessary suffering. The middle class is in a never-ending negotiation for success. The great ones know success and fulfillment are non-negotiable.

▶ **ACTION STEP FOR TODAY**

On a scale of 1 to 7, 7 being highest, how much are you willing to suffer to make your ultimate vision a reality?

133

Champions Learn From Role Models

"Set a goal, not only to follow world-class role models,
but to become a world-class role model."
– Steve Siebold

One of the best-kept secrets of the world class is their ability to use other people's thoughts, ideas, habits and traits as a way to accelerate their own journey to the top. They are savvy enough to know none of us will live long enough to learn all the wisdom of the world from our own experience. Instead, they choose role models who are champions in their fields and learn everything they can from these people. They approach their role models with a beginner's mindset and a humble attitude. This tends to be one of the biggest differences between the upper class and the world class: humility. The upper class tends to be ego-driven and have a high need for wealth and power. Would-be mentors and role models can easily be dissuaded from helping brash, cocky performers with out-of-control egos. The world class has supreme self-confidence only expressed in words to themselves. This inner arrogance is rarely expressed outside their own self-talk. The great ones are able to maintain a spirit of humility and gratitude that spills over from the inside out and covers them with a warm, loving glow. This phenomenon rockets their Rate of Vibration (ROV) to the world-class level. This creates a magnetic attraction others find hard to resist. Role models and mentors love to help performers with this mindset, and their guidance and advice catapult performers years ahead of their ego-driven competition.

▶ **ACTION STEP FOR TODAY**

Identify the most important thing you are trying to accomplish in the next ninety days, and select a role model who has already done it. Learn everything you can about this person, but most of all, their thought processes. When you have this information, pretend you are your role model – with all the confidence and self-assurance of someone who has already succeeded at the task you want to achieve. This technique is the mental equivalent of Clark Kent going into the phone booth and changing into Superman, and it's a fairly common practice of the world class when they're searching for a strategic advantage – especially under pressure.

134

The World Class Believes In The Power Of Self-Understanding

"Ninety percent of the world's woe comes from people not knowing themselves, their abilities, their frailties, and even their real virtues. Most of us go almost all the way through life as complete strangers to ourselves – so how can we know anyone else?"

– Sidney J. Harris, newspaper columnist

Champions are famous for knowing themselves – the good, the bad, and the ugly. While average people choose to selectively view the qualities, thought processes, habits and traits they admire about themselves, the world class prefers a three-dimensional picture. The great ones are masters of self-discovery and personal objectivity because they are always improving themselves. Their commitment to excellence is unyielding, and their focus would alarm average people. The pros often see themselves as performance machines with the goal of figuring out what makes the machine run. When a breakdown occurs, they want to know how to fix it fast and get back on track. The first place this philosophy shows up is in the work or career they select. It's rare to find professional performers doing work they don't enjoy. The great ones invest time in self-introspection until they pinpoint where their interests, talents and unique gifts lie. They know the foundation of world-class performance is loving what you do. The secret is to select a job, career or business you would enjoy, regardless of whether you were paid. The pros know this, and selecting the right vocation is one of their most important tasks. In their personal life, this high level of self-understanding also helps them find and marry the right person. While average people are seeking a mate who stimulates and excites their emotions, the world class is looking for a partner who communicates and connects with their spirit. Many champions describe their spouse as their "soul mate." These are marriages that usually last through thick and thin. On the other hand, when the emotional excitement dies down for amateurs, the relationship loses its attraction. Studies show that 67% of the couples married since 1991 are now divorced. People who have the same core values and see themselves as soul mates have a difficult time being apart. These two examples – work and love – are direct results of the differences in mindset. So, while the middle class is living lives of quiet desperation, the great ones are reaping the rewards of their superior mental habits and philosophies.

▶ **ACTION STEP FOR TODAY**

Make a list of your five most important values and write down why they are so important to you. This simple exercise will get you started down the road of self-understanding, or accelerate the introspective journey you have already begun.

135

The Great Ones Evolve From Success to Significance

"I never wanted to be a successful person. I wanted to be a significant person."

– Nido Qubein, speaker, author, philanthropist

The masses chase success, and often find it elusive as a result of their limited belief system. The few that break through typically make to it the upper-class level of consciousness, where they remain for the rest of their lives. The upper class is driven by ego and power. While some of them build financial fortunes, they often suffer from a lack of meaning and fulfillment in their lives. This is evident by the number of broken relationships many of them experience. In an attempt to gain greater fulfillment, this group is famous for throwing money at their relationship problems and attempting to use their power to coerce their friends and loved ones to their point of view. When this eventually fails, as it must, the upper class doesn't understand how they can be so successful professionally, but not personally. Their egocentric addiction renders them blind to the simple truth that fulfillment and happiness cannot be coerced or purchased. The few that make this discovery are jettisoned to the world class almost overnight, where they trade in their ego-based thoughts for a spirit-filled consciousness. The upper class focuses on success; the world class focuses on significance. The great ones discover what fulfills them first and end up with success as a byproduct. Their secret to a fulfilling life is often through servant leadership to a large group of people who need their help. There is a direct correlation between their level of fulfillment and the magnitude of impact they have on the people they serve. In other words, the more significant the champions become in the lives of others, the more fulfillment they experience, and the more fulfillment they experience, the more energy and effort they invest in other people. The success formula is similar, but requires that the performer help large numbers of people in order to reap large rewards. The irony is that many great performers become successful without ever chasing success. Their journey to fulfillment through helping other people creates success by natural law. By focusing on becoming a significant person in the lives of others, they automatically gain the success that the masses so desperately seek. Their world-class success and fulfillment creates world-class happiness. That's why we call them the great ones.

▶ ACTION STEP FOR TODAY

Ask this critical thinking question: "Am I focusing my energy on becoming successful or significant?"

136

Champions Know Humor Is No Joke

"Comedy makes the human spirit soar."
— Mel Brooks, actor, director

The world class is famous for being the hardest working, hardest playing people on the planet. The upside of their work ethic is success. The downside is stress. This is why the great ones use humor to ease tension and offer a fresh perspective on whatever challenge they may be facing. Champions know the most potent antidote for stress is levity. When the world watched in horror as former U.S. president Ronald Reagan was shot in 1980, the first words the president uttered to his wife were: "Honey, I forgot to duck." The collective tension of an entire nation was instantly lowered by this humorous statement. Professional performers know that humor is no joke when it comes to enhancing their ability to perform in pressure situations. The impact of a simple laugh can make the difference between choking under pressure and breaking a world record. Champions understand the power that humor has on their mind, body and spirit. It's a force for good that many amateurs overlook. While the average performer sees humor as folly, the great ones see it as the ultimate, instant stress reduction tool.

▶ **ACTION STEP FOR TODAY**

Make a commitment to develop a Top 10 Jokes List. Research jokes on the internet, browse for joke books in bookstores, and attend a comedy show. Develop this list as a mental toughness strategy to help you reduce pressure in your everyday life.

▶▶❘ **WORLD-CLASS RESOURCE**

Read Good Clean Jokes, by Bob Philips.

137

The World Class Is Character Conscious

"Be more concerned with your character than your reputation, because your character is what you really are, while your reputation is merely what others think you are."

— John Wooden, Hall of Fame basketball coach, University of California Los Angeles

World-class performers, almost by definition, have rock-solid character. These people are self-reliant and strong, and often have belief systems that reflect their superior self-confidence. Champions take the high road and are known to do what they say they will do. If champions are your friends, you can count on them to show up when things get tough. They won't shy away from or be afraid of adversity. They make deals with other champions on a handshake, and view it as a binding contract. Their world view is that life is what you make it, and the rest is how you take it. Character is what helps world-class performers get through the tough times, and what governs their mighty ambitions. Champions will push only to the limits their character will allow. When their ambitions and drives begin to adversely affect other people, champions pull back. Character is what separates ambitious champions from ambitious criminals. It's a small distinction that makes all the difference in the world.

▶ ACTION STEP FOR TODAY

Make a commitment to always do what you say you will do, no matter what it takes. Put your commitment in writing. This philosophy separates you from 95% of the population, and will enhance all of your relationships.

▶▶I WORLD-CLASS RESOURCE

If you have children, check out www.charactercounts.org

138

The World Class Builds On Support

*"Lots of people want to ride with you in the limo,
but what you want is someone who will take the
bus with you when the limo breaks down."*
— *Oprah Winfrey, television personality*

While many amateur thinkers believe it's them against the world, professionals rely on their emotional support teams to help them sustain focus through the peaks and valleys of performance. Their support teams are made up of people who love them unconditionally, no matter whether they are winning or losing. Champions use mentor teams and coaches to push them to greater heights, and support teams to help them recover emotionally when the going gets tough and they become emotionally drained. Even the toughest performers in the world need emotional support from time to time, and they tap this resource on a regular basis to avoid the worst enemy of any great performer: burnout. Burnout is the brain's way of telling you it's stressed and strained for the time being, and its way of shutting you down is to rob you of any measure of enthusiasm you ever had for the activity involved. The only way to fully recover from mental burnout is by getting away from the activity for an extended period of time. In order to avoid burnout, the great ones spend time with their families, friends and other support team members that help them recover before it occurs. The support team serves as the champion's physical, mental and spiritual oasis on their way to the top.

▶ **ACTION STEP FOR TODAY**

Make a list of the people who love you unconditionally, and make a commitment to speak with or visit them on a regular basis.

139

Champions Have A World Class Work Ethic

"Amateurs hope; professionals work."
— Garson Kanin, 1912-1999, writer

Amateurs work just hard enough to escape being fired. Their belief system demands they be compensated for every action they take on the job. If they can be over-compensated, that's even better. The pros have the exact opposite belief. The only way you'll ever out-work one of the great ones is to become one. They know there's no such thing as over-compensation, at least not in the long term. The pros know that a free-economy marketplace will always correct itself. They also know the marketplace will richly reward a world-class work ethic with an endless stream of opportunities. This work ethic is the reason so many immigrants come to the free world and become millionaires. They remember where they came from and what it took to get them to the land of the free. They're so grateful for the opportunity to work hard that no one can convince them to slow down. Nido Qubein, a Lebanese immigrant, came to America with only a dream and a world-class work ethic and built an empire. Immigrants are four times as likely to become millionaires as American-born citizens. This startling statistic boils down to one thing: a world-class work ethic.

▶ **ACTION STEP FOR TODAY**

On a scale of 1 to 7, 7 being highest, rate your work ethic. If you score less than a 5, upgrade your commitment to work.

▶▶▌ **WORLD-CLASS RESOURCE**

Invest in a copy of Stairway to Success, by Nido Qubein. This book will take you inside the mind of this magnificent entrepreneur. Visit www.nidoqubein.com

140

The World Class Dreams Of The Future, Yet Lives In The Present

"Your experience of yesterday should never set your foundation of expectation for what you can accomplish in the future. Yesterdays lessons are the most effective fertilizer for tomorrow's victories."

– John Terhune CEO, Rainmaker Consulting Services

My late business partner, Bill Gove, once said, "Steve, the only thing significant about the past is how it affects us in the present and the future. It holds no power other than that." The poverty-, working-, and middle-class levels of consciousness have a tendency to be fixated on the past. Their mindset is: "If only this or that would have happened . . . If only I could have done this or that." Amateurs are always looking in the rear view mirror, wishing things were different. Instead of learning from the lessons of their past, they assume a victim-based mindset and tend to wallow in their sorrow. Playing the victim gives the amateur an excuse for losing. The world class rarely looks back to the past except when they're feeling nostalgic. The pros know the clock is running. The great ones are acutely aware of their mortality. With this mindset, the pro doesn't have the time or inclination to look back. The great ones are focused on "living in the now." They leave living in the past to the amateurs.

▶ **ACTION STEP FOR TODAY**

Let go of your past and focus exclusively on the present and the future.

141
The Great Ones Know How To Say "No"

"Do not squander time, for that is the stuff life is made of."
– Benjamin Franklin, 1706-1790, inventor, statesman

World-class performenrs are ruthless with their time. This behavior stems from their awareness of their limited time on the planet. They view time as their most valuable resource. As pros become more successful, they have to say "no" more often. Additional projects, favors and various burdens threaten to eat away their time. Amateurs tend to believe they have more time left than they actually do. The thought of their mortality is too great a prospect to face squarely. Amateurs are masters in the art of self-deception and psychological delusion. Reality is too harsh for their fragile psyches to endure. The world class is generous, yet highly selective, with their time. They seldom feel guilty about saying "no," even when they are criticized by amateurs for being uncaring and selfish. Champions operate from an internal frame of reference and tend to value their own opinion above that of others'. Amateurs see this as arrogance; pros see it as self-confidence. The middle class is highly vulnerable to the opinions of others, and tend to say "yes" to anything they are asked. This behavior suggests a generous spirit, but is more likely the manifestation of the amateur addiction to love and acceptance from others.

▶ **ACTION STEP FOR TODAY**

Identify an activity that is not giving you the results or satisfaction you thought it would. Make a commitment to discontinue it. Get in the habit of saying "no" more often in order to protect your precious time.

142

Champions Are Not Addicted To The Approval Of Others

"I am responsible to my employees, customers, and business associates; to be honest, sincere, and to act with integrity . . . but I am not responsible for their attitudes or behavior towards me. I hope they like me. It's more pleasant that way, but if not, it's not my problem."

— Bill Gove, 1912-2001, the father of professional speaking

Bill Gove used to speak to audiences around the world about what he called "the most debilitating addiction." Bill was convinced this addiction was worse than an addiction to drugs, booze or sex. Bill called it "the addiction to the approval of others." This addiction stems from believing, "I won't be loved or accepted unless others approve of my behavior." It's conformity at any cost. Amateurs operate from an outer frame of reference which values the opinions of others above their own. This is why the middle class makes lousy leaders – and even worse salespeople. Amateurs tend to live their lives in first gear for fear of psychological abandonment. The aggregate cost to companies hiring salespeople and executive leaders could be substantially reduced if they would hire for consciousness rather than compliance. Southwest Airlines says they hire for attitude and train for skills. I'd like to upgrade that to "hire for consciousness and train for skills."

▶ **ACTION STEP FOR TODAY**

On a scale of 1 to 7, 7 being highest, how high is your need to be approved and validated by other people? Next, ask your spouse or best friend to rate you on the same scale, and then compare answers.

143

The World Class Loves Liberty

"Liberty means responsibility. That is why most men dread it."
– George Bernard Shaw, 1856-1950, author and critic

While the middle class may take their liberties for granted, the world class sees it as one of their greatest assets. Liberty: the right to act, believe, or express yourself in the manner of your choosing. The great ones know their opportunity to become great begins with the freedom to choose and create their own destiny. The middle-class consciousness doesn't hold liberty in such high regard, because they don't believe they have that much to lose. They are unaware that their liberty, combined with their ability to upgrade their programming, has the potential to catapult them into world-class consciousness. As a result, they remain mentally bound to mediocrity. They are searching the world for gold, not knowing it is right in their own backyard. Champions are much different, and that's why they tend to be happier, more successful and more fulfilled. Their world is filled with love and abundance, while the middle class continues to operate from fear and scarcity. Without the gift of liberty, the great ones might never discover their true potential. Meanwhile, the middle class has everything they need to become everything they can become, yet they choose to play it safe.

▶ **ACTION STEP FOR TODAY**

Ask this critical thinking question: "Am I taking full advantage of the liberty that so many of my fellow countrymen fought and died for?"

144

The Great Ones Seek Solitude

"Periods of wholesome laziness, after days of energetic effort, will wonderfully tone up the mind and body. It does not involve loss of time, since after a day of complete rest and quietness, you will return to your regular occupation with renewed interest and vigor."
– Grenville Kleiser, 1868-1953, author

The masses don't need to be overly concerned about rest and recovery, because they're not pushing themselves much beyond the typical routines of everyday life. The average American watches 1,669 hours of television per year. This activity is more of an escape than a recovery strategy. Most champions are aware that, due to their emotional nature, human beings need recovery strategies if they are going to be at their best, day in and day out. One of the most popular among champions is solitude. The simple act of getting away and getting quiet creates more space between their thoughts and helps them escape the bondage of excessive cognition. When it comes to getting big results, average performers often believe working harder and longer is the answer. Champions often cut back on traditional work time to allow their creative mind to operate at greater capacity. This working-smarter strategy blends in beautifully in the 21st century, which is quickly becoming known as "The Age of the Mind." Many of world's highest-paid people are able to tap into the vast resources of their creative minds to produce products and services that solve the problems of the masses. This level of creative thought requires significant intellectual energy, which must be followed by intellectual rest and recovery. The great ones know the power of a quiet mind, and many invest time in solitude on a regular basis. They recognize the performance value of a rested mind, body and spirit.

▶ **ACTION STEP FOR TODAY**

Just for today, carve out at least 20 minutes of your workday to get away from everyone and get quiet. This simple recovery strategy will do wonders for you if you make it a habit.

145

Champions Are Happily Dissatisfied

> "Show me a thoroughly satisfied man –
> and I will show you a failure."
> – *Thomas Edison, 1847-1931, inventor*

Average people have been labeled "somewhat dissatisfied." This level of dissatisfaction probably says more about their lack of belief in themselves than it does about their feelings of contentment. If a person earns $50,000 per year and believes he has the ability to earn $60,000 per year, a low level of dissatisfaction with $50,000 likely results. On the other hand, a person earning $50,000 a year who believes he can earn $500,000 is very dissatisfied with his results. World-class performers understand the power of healthy dissatisfaction, and are in a never-ending quest to raise their levels of expectation and upgrade their beliefs. While average people believe, "If you don't expect much, you won't be disappointed," champions believe, "The only way I'll be disappointed is if I don't take risks and give it my all." This is a classic example of how directly opposite philosophies drive these two groups. The results are obvious. The middle class ends up playing it safe in order to gain comfort and security; the world class becomes the movers and shakers. A good description of the world class is "happily dissatisfied." The great ones are in the habit of playing the game of life without a net, and it all begins with the pain of being dissatisfied with their current results.

▶ **ACTION STEP FOR TODAY**

If you're satisfied in every area of your life, ask why. Are you content because you are truly content, or are you content because you don't believe you are capable of accomplishing or becoming more?

146

The World Class Masters Time Management

"Even as we speak, jealous time flees—seize this day, and put little faith in tomorrow."

– Horace, philosopher

Average people hate Monday, refer to Wednesday as "hump day" and "Thank God it's Friday." On the other end of the spectrum, champions enjoy all of it. The middle-class consciousness lives for the weekend; the world class lives in the now. Champions use their belief in themselves and their ferocious ambition to create the work and home life they desire; so there is no need to wish time away. This is one of the biggest secrets of the high achievers. Average people search for security, while champions discover their life's vision and purpose. When they discover the work they love so much they would do it for free, they embark on the journey of what Dr. Abraham Maslow referred to as "self-actualization," or becoming all one can be. This is the true secret of their success. They are using time, rather than allowing time to use them.

In other words, the great ones understand that no matter how successful they become, time is the one resource they cannot create or purchase. Therefore, time becomes their most valued prize. Since they love their work and home lives, they tend to outwork, outplay, and (some would say) outlive their middle-class counterparts. The great ones know that no one can truly manage time, yet everyone can manage activities. With that in mind, the great ones surround themselves with activities they love so they are sure to get the most fulfillment out of the time they have.

▶ **ACTION STEP FOR TODAY**

Ask yourself how much time you are wishing away in anticipation of a more pleasurable or fulfilling time. Look at your life with honesty: is it possible to stop investing time in activities you like and exchange them for activities you love?

147

Champions Follow The Results Matrix

"Sales results say more about the salesperson's belief system than it does about her sales skills. What the salesperson believes about her product, company, herself and her prospect has a greater impact on her results than anything she learned in sales training. Beliefs control behavior, and behavior creates results. The real secret to increasing sales is upgrading the salespersons belief system, and it all begins with programming."

— Steve Siebold

Average performers tend to take a hit or miss approach to attracting success, fulfillment and happiness into their lives. Professional performers follow the formula known as the Results Matrix. (Some are aware they're following it, others are not.) The great ones believe the ultimate prize is happiness, and that happiness is the result of success and fulfillment. They further believe success and fulfillment are created by the appropriate habits, actions and behaviors, which are dictated by a performer's level of consciousness. The performer's level of consciousness is created by their beliefs, and their beliefs are created by their own programming, which is the manifestation of the language and mental pictures they use with themselves and others. The Results Matrix works for any level you want to attain, and it all begins with making a decision on what level of words and pictures you will use on a regular basis. The great ones decide to go pro and immediately upgrade their language and visualization to the world-class level. After this change has been turned into a habit, it's only a matter of time before a mental domino effect begins and the performer starts to achieve world-class results. It's such a simple formula for world-class happiness that most of us miss it. As speaker Jim Rohn says, "It's easy to do, and easy not to do."

▶ **ACTION STEP FOR TODAY**

Review the Results Matrix and decide what level of happiness you wish to attain. Your choices are Poverty class, Working class, Middle class, Upper class, and World class. Next, begin the process of upgrading your language and mental pictures that you use with yourself and others.

RESULTS MATRIX

(__) Class LANGUAGE and VISUALIZATION creates(__) Class Programming,

(__) Class PROGRAMMING creates(__) Class BELIEFS,

(__) Class BELIEFS create (__) Class CONSCIOUSNESS,

(__) Class CONSCIOUSNESS creates (__) Class
HABITS, ACTIONS and BEHAVIORS,

(__) Class HABITS, ACTIONS and BEHAVIORS create
(__) Class SUCCESS and FULFILLMENT,

(__) Class SUCCESS and FULFILLMENT creates
(__) Class HAPPINESS. (The ultimate prize)

148

Champions Avoid Delusion

"The wise men of antiquity, when they wished to make the
whole world peaceful and happy, first put their own States into
proper order. Before putting their States into proper order, they
regulated their own families. Before regulating their families,
they regulated themselves. Before regulating themselves, they
tried to be sincere in their thoughts. Before being sincere in their
thoughts, they tried to see things exactly as they really were."

– Confucius, 551 B.C.E.-479 B.C.E., philosopher

American culture is inundated by devices of delusion. How
many of us are honest with ourselves about our health? Today,
65% of the American population is overweight, and little less than
half of this group is considered obese. Ask someone who needs
to lose weight how much they think they need to lose in order to
reach their ideal weight. You'll likely get an answer that's half the
amount they really need to lose. How about in the area of money?
Most people have little or no wealth and are ninety days from
living on the street, yet they have a wallet full of credit cards that
creates an illusion of wealth. As a result, they don't do anything to
change their circumstances. The same is true in relationships. Millions of marriages project the illusion of happiness when, in truth,
they are held together only by economic necessity. The world class,
however, operates from objective reality. They start with the facts
and build on them. Ask champions how much weight they need
to lose, and you'll get an accurate number. Ask about money, and
you'll find they take it very seriously. They know how much they
have and how to leverage it to get more. Ask about their relationships, and you'll find most of them put a great deal of time
and effort into keeping their relationships strong and solid. The
great ones tend to stay on top of their key relationships and keep

close tabs on problems or issues as they occur. The world class has superior problem-solving skills because they have the courage to build their lives on a solid foundation of objective reality.

▶ ACTION STEP FOR TODAY

Take stock of your life. Look at the critical areas of your life through the eyes of objective reality and determine where you stand. Look at your health, finances, relationships, career or business, spiritual development, recreational activities, and any other area that's important to you. On a scale of 1 to 7, 7 being outstanding and 1 being lousy, how are you doing? Rate yourself and then create a written plan to improve in the next ninety days.

149

Champions Feed Their Vision And Starve Their Fear

"The world you desire can be won. It exists,
it is real, it is possible, it is yours."
– Ayn Rand, 1905-1982, author, philosopher

All great philosophers seem to agree that human beings become what they think about most of the time. For this reason, the world class creates compelling visions written with great attention to detail and fueled by emotion, and then they think about their vision all the time. The great ones seem to go through four stages of mental evolution after creating a world-class vision: The first stage brings them increased mental clarity, which occurs as a result of putting their dreams on paper. The second stage is an intensified focus on the vision, which occurs as a result of the performer thinking about the vision morning, noon and night. The third stage turns their intensified focus into a burning desire, which is often fueled by the frustration of seeing and believing the vision is reality on the mental plane but not yet on the physical plane. Champions often develop incredible visualization and self-talk skills that convince the subconscious the vision they project on the movie screen of their mind is real, when at the same time the performers' conscious mind knows it's not. This creates what psychologists call 'cognitive dissonance', or two thoughts (cognitions) that are inconsistent. Since the human mind hates to be inconsistent, it drives the performer to take action and make the vision a reality. This success-driven behavior creates the final stage, which occurs when the vision turns into an obsession. Most of the time it's a healthy obsession, which means the performer is thinking, strategizing and moving closer to her vision every day. When stage four kicks in, failure is no longer an option. The champion will do whatever it takes to manifest the vision. The great ones fuel their obsession by only thinking positive thoughts about their vision, and these thoughts create psychological, physiological and spiritual energy. At this stage they are no longer willing to entertain thoughts of fear, and will shelter themselves from anything or anyone who approaches them speaking the language of scarcity. In essence, the great ones feed their vision and starve their fear.

▶ ACTION STEP FOR TODAY

Just for today, decide that you will only think thoughts of love and abundance, especially as they relate to your vision. Refuse to entertain any thoughts of fear or scarcity, and shelter yourself from anything or anyone that brings you negative energy.

4 LEVELS OF VISION

1. Increased Mental Clarity - *Excitement Phase*

2. Intensified Focus - *Season of Pain*

3. Burning Desire fueled by Frustration and Vision - *Season of Pain*

4. Healthy Obsession - *Knowing Phase*

150

The Great Ones Are Powerful Public Speakers

"If I went back to college again, I'd concentrate on two areas: learning to write and learning to speak before an audience. Nothing in life is more important than the ability to communicate effectively."

– Gerald R. Ford, U.S. President

According to the polls, the greatest fear of average people is speaking in public. In direct contrast, the world class has used public speaking to persuade and influence people for thousands of years. The power to lead and build support through public speaking is a direct result that is based on the fear it represents to the masses. Think about it: 95% of the average audience listening to a speaker is in awe of the perceived courage and talent it takes to stand up and deliver a speech. This sense of awe creates a magnified impact on listeners and carries far more credibility than a person trying to persuade someone one-on-one. The great ones know this phenomenon exists, so they master the art of public speaking. They speak at every opportunity and seek training and coaching along the way. The introverted and shy champions battle incredible levels of fear to become proficient at public speaking, yet they forge ahead, knowing they are relegated to lower places unless they learn to master this skill. Their vision won't allow this to happen. Champions do whatever it takes to master this critical skill. The result is supreme confidence and the ability to communicate more effectively, without fear, to one or one thousand at a time.

▶ **ACTION STEP FOR TODAY**

Decide to become an excellent public speaker. Get training and coaching. Visit www.speechworkshop.com and enroll in the Bill Gove Speech Workshop. Join a Toastmasters club in your area. Visit www.toastmasters.org

---

151

The World Class Develops Emotional Intelligence

"The secret of success is not what they taught you in school. What matters most is not I.Q., not a business-school degree, not even technical know-how or years of expertise. The single most important factor in job performance and advancement is emotional intelligence."
– Daniel Goleman, author

The middle class believes formal education is the most impor-tant key to success, yet studies show a person's level of emo-tional intelligence is far more significant. The world class places a high value on their ability to influence other people through their charm, charisma and emotional maturity. While the masses appeal to logic, the world class realizes human beings are emo-tionally driven creatures who respond far better to emotionally charged words, gestures and actions. Champions place relation-ships above all else in their interactions with others. The middle class goes to great lengths to deny emotion is at the root of their habits, actions and behaviors, although the evidence clearly shows emotional creatures operate primarily from emotion. The masses believe their decisions are almost always grounded in logic and fact. The great ones know people buy with emotion and justify with logic. This one difference in philosophy has a tremendous impact on the results the two groups realize, as well as on their corresponding approach to self-improvement. The middle class chases more formal education; the world class seeks to improve their level of emotional intelligence by studying human behavior and its impact on the people around them. Champions are always studying emotional intelligence topics such as psychology, sociology, philosophy, self-help, spirituality and etiquette. It propels their emotional and interpersonal skills, and as a result, their success and fulfillment.

▶ **ACTION STEP FOR TODAY**

Develop your emotional intelligence. Start by rating yourself on a scale of 1 to 7, 7 being the highest, of how emotionally intelligent you are right now.

EMOTION AND LOGIC HAVE AN INVERSE RELATIONSHIP

As Emotion Goes Up, Logic Goes Down

▶▶❘ **WORLD-CLASS RESOURCE**

Invest in Emotional Intelligence, by Daniel Goleman. This book will take you, step-by-step, through the process of developing world-class emotional intelligence. If you're a manager who's interested in training your team in this area, visit www.mentaltoughnessuniversity.com

152

The World Class Forms Brain Trusts

"I use not only all of the brains I have, but all I can borrow."
— *Woodrow Wilson, 1856-1924, U.S. President*

Amateur performers are fixated on their perceived level of intelligence, just as most of us were taught to be in school. They spend a good part of their lives secretly fearing the world will find out they are not intelligent enough. Professional performers operate from a higher mental plane. They see intelligence as something that can be assembled through a team, whose collective intelligence would surpass Einstein, Freud and Marx. The egoless champions assemble a mentor team to help them solve problems, and to create new and innovative ways of doing things. Since champions don't care about who gets the credit, they lead, yet surrender to the collective brainpower of the team. Average people feel they must solve all their problems using their own intelligence, or risk being viewed as nonessential or obsolete. Fear keeps the middle class from harnessing the power of the brain trust. Champions carefully construct this mentor team brain trust and serve as leaders and facilitators. Many of the greatest minds in the world come together each year at a think tank called the Aspen Institute, in Aspen, Colorado. Some of society's biggest problems are discussed and masterminded there, far from the media and the rest of the world. The great ones are smart enough to engage other people to assist them in accomplishing their goals.

▶ **ACTION STEP FOR TODAY**

Create or join a mastermind group of intelligent, engaged and powerful people who can help you get what you want.

153

The Great Ones Are Obsessed With Strategic Advantages

"The ultimate strategic advantage in business is surrounding yourself with a team of world-class performers who are committed to the cause. If you're looking for an unfair advantage over your competition, look no farther than your people."

– George Madiou, speaker, author

World-class performers are always looking for an edge, an ace in the hole – something to give them the slightest advantage over their opponent or competition. Champions realize the difference between the good and the great can usually be measured in inches, rather than feet. They know it's the little things that make the difference. Examples include Federal Express, pummeling the competition by guaranteeing overnight delivery to any location in the continental United States. Another example is Domino's Pizza, delivering in 30 minutes or less. The major difference we've found between average people and the world class is that, while average people would love to have a strategic advantage, champions are borderline obsessed with finding it. Some of the best competitive-advantage ideas come to champions in the middle of the night. While the masses dream of winning the lottery, champions dream of the one little add-on detail that takes them to a whole new level of success.

► **ACTION STEP FOR TODAY**

Write down one strategic advantage you can implement in your job/business immediately that will make a difference. It doesn't have to be anything big, because when you get in the habit of doing this everyday, the little things add up to a make a significant difference.

154

The World Class Reframes Painful Past Experiences

"It's never too late to have a wonderful childhood."
— *Larry Wilson, founder, Wilson Learning Corporation*

Champions believe the only thing relevant about their past is how it affects their present and future. The middle-class consciousness bases many beliefs on the events of the past, yet the world class knows the past does not equal the future. Champions are masters at placing new, empowering meanings on the struggles of the past. Average people invest a lot of time living in the past and wishing things were different. The great ones know that, without the trouble and turbulence they experienced in the past, they would not be where they are today. This attitude creates mental harmony and fosters good feelings about an otherwise troublesome set of memories. Good memories of the past are not an issue for anyone; it's the tough times that reveal the level of the performer. The great ones share the philosophy that everything happens for a reason. This allows them to reframe events they originally perceived as negative. This is another example of how champions use the concept of truth vs. fact. The past event is fact. How they interpret the past event is truth. Knowing they cannot change the facts of the past, champions instead alter their interpretation of the facts. This mental tool enables them to transform the pain of the past into a positive catalyst for growth in the future.

▶ **ACTION STEP FOR TODAY**

Review the 3 most difficult adversities you listed in Action Step 12, and ask yourself how these events contributed to your future success or fulfillment. Reframe each event into a memory with the potential to serve you in the future.

155

Champions Know Their Brains' Primary Purpose

"What a thing means is to an unknowable extent determined by what we think it means."
– *Joseph Chilton Pearce*

The great ones know the human brain's primary purpose is the preservation of the mind and body. When an event occurs, the brain asks three questions: 1) What is it? 2) What does it mean? 3) What do I do? The answers determine how the performer responds to any given situation. The secret that champions have discovered is that what an event means is all based on the subjective perception of the performer, and is therefore subject to change. If you change the perception of the event, you automatically change the brain's response to it. An example would be a salesperson facing rejection day in and day out. The middle-class thinker perceives this rejection to mean pain and suffering; the world class perceives it as completely necessary to justify being paid a large salary and healthy commissions. If the champion had the opportunity to remove rejection from the equation, she would refuse to do it, knowing that the job would no longer be worth as much in the marketplace. Instead, she alters her perceptions to empower her as a professional performer. The same scenario could apply to someone in the middle of a divorce. The average thinker perceives the divorce as a personal failure; the world-class thinker sees it as a learning experience that will make him tougher and wiser. Which performer is right? Both, because perception, to an emotional creature, is reality. It sometimes appears that the masses allow themselves to suffer for the sake of suffering, when all they have to do is make a subtle shift in their perceptions and reprogram what any given event means to them. While both experiencing the same event, the amateurs are suffering while the pros are dancing in the streets. The only difference lies in the way they manage and manipulate their emotions.

▶ ACTION STEP FOR TODAY

Identify the three most important events that are currently happening in your life, and ask this critical thinking question: "What do I think they mean, and is my perception of these events helping or hurting me?"

156

The World Class Focuses On 'The Why'

"Send the harmony of a great desire vibrating through every fiber of your being. Find a task that will call forth your faith, your courage, your perseverance, and your spirit of sacrifice. Keep your hands and your soul clean, and your conquering current will flow freely."

—Thomas Dreier, American Author

World-class thinkers know that when it comes to manifesting their ultimate visions, the real question that must be answered is not the how-to, but the why. In other words, odds are that someone, somewhere, already knows how to do whatever the champion wants to do, and can most likely be tapped as a mentor for assistance. The critical thinking question is "Why do I want this vision to become reality?" The intensity of emotion in which this question is answered will determine whether the dream comes alive or dies. If your house was burning down, would you risk your life to save the furniture? Probably not, but if your kids were trapped inside the house, would you risk your life trying to save them? Of course. The point is we will do anything if the stakes are high enough, if we have a big enough reason why. World-class thinkers know this and capitalize on it. While middle-class thinkers are scaling back their goals and dreams because they don't know how to accomplish them, world-class thinkers are soul searching for their emotional motivators. The salesperson who dreams of winning the company trip to Maui and being recognized on stage in front of his family and peers. The manager who envisions leading her team to record-breaking sales in order to prove to herself that she is as good as she knew she was, even though her stepfather told her that she would never amount to anything. Champions know the secret to world-class motivation lies in emotion. The great ones decide what they want, and more importantly, why they want it. They know all benefits come down to an emotion that we are trying to create though our goals and dreams, so they invest a lot of mental energy attempting to identify what emotion they are really after. Once they discover it, the fight to make their vision a reality is over before it begins. Obstacles and setbacks are no match for a visionary driven by raw emotion. Ordinary people are transformed into extraordinary performers who no longer recognize failure as an option. The power of emotional motivation is unmistakable, yet only the champions invest the time to tap into it.

▶ ACTION STEP FOR TODAY

Make a commitment to clearly identify what is driving you to achieve your life's vision. The five most popular emotional motivators in our Mental Toughness University Program are:

1) Religious/Spiritual Beliefs
2) Children/Family
3) Desire to prove oneself to oneself
4) Desire to prove oneself to others
5) General recognition/validation

157

The Great Ones Are Critical Thinkers

*"Critical thinkers do not just drift through life,
subject to every message they hear; they think through
their choices and make conscious decisions."*
– Sherry Diestler, author

There are five basic levels of thinking we engage in at any given time: The lowest level is unengaged – going through the motions without really thinking about what we're doing. The next level up is negative thinking, which is rooted in a fear- and scarcity-based consciousness. We look for the negative in every situation. Next is neutral thinking, which is neither positive nor negative. Neutral thinking implies a lack of energy at best, indifference at worst. This is the thinking pattern of those who would like to be more successful and are aware of how to do it, but can't be bothered to invest much thought energy into the process. Neutral thinking is one of the hallmarks of the middle class. The next level is positive thinking, which often manifests positive results. This mindset is rooted in love and abundance, but is sometimes blinded by emotion. The mantra of the positive thinker is "look for the good in everything." It's a good place to start, unless you're standing in the middle of a highway and a truck is headed toward you at ninety miles an hour and positive thinking tells you the truck will swerve out of your path! Positive thinking is a good foundation, yet it's no match for the world-class philosophy of critical thinking. Critical thinkers use specific criteria to evaluate their reasoning and make decisions, unclouded by emotion. The critical thinker reasons that the speeding truck driver may not see him and decides to move out of the way. Critical thinking has been called the most difficult work in the age in which we now live: the Age of the Mind.

▶ **ACTION STEP FOR TODAY**

When you care about something, what type of thinker are you? How is your level of thinking impacting your current results?

THE FIVE LEVELS OF THINKING

Critical Thinking (World Class)

Positive Thinking (Upper Class)

Neutral (Middle Class)

Negative Thinking (Working Class)

Non-Engagement (Poverty Class)

▶▶I **WORLD-CLASS RESOURCE**

For further study, read Becoming a Critical Thinker, by Sherry Diestler.

158

Champions Live By The Law Of Attraction

"We attract into our lives whatever we give our energy, focus, and attention to, whether wanted or unwanted."

– Michael J. Losier, author

One of the most significant secrets of the world class is their thorough understanding that we attract into our lives what we are, not what we want. The law of attraction has been written about for thousands of years. Secular wisdom defines it as the power of the subconscious, directed by our dominant thoughts, that attracts people, events and circumstances into our lives to fulfill our visions. Spiritual leaders argue that dominant thoughts and prayers attract these same people, events and circumstances through divine intervention. Whatever your belief, the one thing all thought leaders seem to agree on is this: the law of attraction exists and manifests our dominant thoughts on the physical plane. The great ones know what they think about or give energy to will grow. It doesn't matter if it's negative, positive or neutral. The law operates without judgment. This is the reason average people barely get by, while the world class lives in abundance. Thoughts are simply a series of vibrations that grow when supplied with energy. Champions can lose everything on the physical plane and gain it back very quickly just by bathing their minds in thoughts of love and abundance. These thoughts lead to belief, and belief leads to behavior which creates results. The middle class often misses the concept, while the great ones reap the rewards by obeying this law.

▶ ACTION STEP FOR TODAY

Examine the major areas of your life and identify your dominant thoughts in each area. If you're unsure what you're thinking in these areas, check your results. Your results are the manifestation of your dominant thoughts over a period of time. If you wish to change your results, change your dominant thoughts. Just for today, select one area of your life and write down three new thoughts you are going to condition yourself to hold in your mind. Do this for thirty days and monitor your results.

▶▶ WORLD-CLASS RESOURCE

Pick up Law of Attraction, by Michael J. Losier. This book is a quick read and gets to the point fast.

159

The Great Ones Use Mentors

"The ultimate source of information, and the whole world's living wisdom, lies in the minds of others . . . all you have to do is ask."
— Walter Hailey, 1928-2003, entrepreneur, speaker

The masses are content to acquire knowledge, information and wisdom the old-fashioned way – from experience. Champions are different. They believe in working smarter, not harder. This means learning from mentors and coaches, who have the ability to accelerate the process exponentially. My late friend and client, Walter Hailey, the famous entrepreneur from Texas, used to say the secret to his success was his ability to "copy genius." Instead of investing years in the school of hard knocks, the world class often reaches their heights by standing on the shoulders of giants. Champions are famous for building mentor teams who are already where they want to be. Corporations call this group a board of directors. Individuals call it a mentor team. Mentor teams guide, teach, advise and encourage performers to think bigger and reach higher than ever before. They often provide specialized knowledge and contacts linked to the area of life in which the performer needs assistance. The overall task of mentors is to help performers raise their level of awareness and expectation. Mentors are continually prodding and pushing champions beyond their comfort zone. The major advantage of the mentor team is the speed with which it accelerates the performer's growth. While average people expand their consciousness at a steady rate, the mentor team demands rocket-like acceleration from their charges. The mentor team is an ace in the hole for champions.

► **ACTION STEP FOR TODAY**

Make a list of the five most successful people you know and make a commitment to use the 'copy genius' philosophy with them.

▶▶▮ **WORLD-CLASS RESOURCE**

Read Breaking the No Barrier, by Walter Hailey. I first read it in 1999 and I've read it five times since. Walter Hailey was one of the great business tycoons in the history of Texas, and credited most of his success to learning from mentors. This book takes you behind the scenes and inside the mind of a master thinker.

160
Champions Are Congruent

> "Congruency between your vision and your action will determine whether you are a visionary or a daydreamer."
>
> – *Steve Siebold*

As you know, one of the defining characteristics of champions is that they know exactly what they want, why they want it, and how to get it. Their actions are congruent with the size and scope of their vision. While average performers wish for the stars, they rarely back up their big dreams with world-class action. Champions know that the road to uncommon success and emotional fulfillment is paved with all-out, massive action. This congruency integrates their belief with their behavior. The masses have retained a set of limiting beliefs from childhood, and continue to have these beliefs reinforced and validated by others around them. The likelihood of them achieving outstanding results is slim to none, unless they are exposed to a higher level of awareness and recognize it. To determine the size of the champion, check for congruency between their vision and their habits, actions and behaviors. If they are incongruent, performers have one of two choices: upgrade their habits, actions and behaviors or reduce the size and scope of their vision. This congruency model is what world-class coaches have used for years to keep their performers on track. It's the reason creating a detailed, emotionally charged vision is the first step in the mental toughness process.

▶ **ACTION STEP FOR TODAY**

Give yourself a reality check to see if your habits, actions and behaviors are congruent with the size and scope of your vision. If they are congruent, move forward knowing that you have a legitimate shot at making your vision a reality. If they are not congruent, make the choice today: Upgrade your habits, actions and behaviors or reduce the size and scope of your vision. The choice is yours.

161

The Great Ones Seek Fulfillment

"People want riches; they need fulfillment."
– Bob Conklin, author

While the masses are programmed to believe success is the secret to happiness, the world class knows this is a myth. Many of them learned this lesson the hard way, from experience. They worked day and night to become successful, and when they arrived, they found it a hollow victory. Many discovered they had the equation backwards. What they should have been doing was seeking fulfillment instead of success, because success almost always follows fulfillment. The best example of this is the secret weapon of the great ones: They love what they do. They don't like it – they love it, and that slight distinction makes all the difference. Loving what you do and how you live your life is the foundation of fulfillment. It's a lot easier to be successful when you are leading a deeply fulfilling life. Fulfillment is a magnet for success. It creates an extremely high level of vibration, because it's rooted in a love-based consciousness. This is why the rich get richer. It's the law of attraction. Success breeds success. Fulfillment breeds fulfillment and attracts success. You can be rich and miserable, but you can't be fulfilled and miserable. Knowing this, the great ones create visions that focus on fulfillment, and manifest success as a byproduct. This one subtle difference in philosophy is what separates the upper class from the world class. The upper class is often fabulously rich, powerful and successful. Some are even billionaires, yet all their money and power can't seem to open the door to happiness. It never will, because the door was never locked.

▶ **ACTION STEP FOR TODAY**

Ask this critical thinking question: "Am I chasing success or seeking fulfillment?" If you're chasing success, can you shift your strategy to seeking fulfillment, knowing success will follow? Do you love what you do for a living so much you would do it for free? If not, what would you do if you had your choice? (Hint: you do!)

162

Champions Escape Excessive Cognition

"Experts believe each of us can tap into our own islands of savant intelligence that are simply overwhelmed by everyday cognition."
– *Scientific American Mind magazine*

The enemy of creativity and clarity is excessive cognition, or having too many thoughts to process at the same time. The old cliché, "you can't see the forest for the trees" applies when this occurs. Cognitive overload is a major problem for many leaders, but not for the world class. Champions know we are living in the age of the mind, where operating with optimal clarity is critical. This is the reason they schedule time to get away and be alone with their thoughts. Amateur thinkers see this as vacation time or time off, but the pros know it's completely different. Investing in solitude gives performers a chance to slow their thought processes and elevate their consciousness in order to gain perspective. When champions' minds are clear and focused, they turn their power to creating new solutions to current problems. The great ones know their single greatest asset is their ability to think. They do whatever it takes to make sure their minds are fresh, rested and clear. One of the most powerful tools gaining popularity with world-class leaders is the flotation tank, a sensory deprivation tool that isolates the mind from external stimulation. It's an enclosed chamber, about the size of a closet, completely dark and soundproof. Inside is a tub, filled with ten inches of water mixed with Epsom salts, in which a person can float. After an hour, the performer emerges, refreshed and renewed. The great ones are open to anything that will give them an edge in their thinking. While the masses focus on exploring outer space, the great ones explore their inner space. This nonlinear approach to thinking and problem solving is misunderstood by the masses, who still believe the key to getting better results is working harder. Champions know thinking is the real answer, and they are committed to keeping their minds fresh and clear.

▶ ACTION STEP FOR TODAY

Schedule time to isolate yourself for twenty to thirty minutes every day for the next week, and take note of how it impacts your ability to think clearly.

▶▶▎ WORLD-CLASS RESOURCE

The most valuable book I've read on this topic is The Book of Floating, by Michael Hutchison. If you're interested in learning more about how to use sensory deprivation to reduce excessive cognition and explore your consciousness, get a copy of this amazing book.

163

The Great Ones Are Masters Of Follow Up

"The average person makes lofty promises to people and is rarely heard from again. The leader makes those same promises and over delivers."

– Bill Gove, 1912-2001, the father of professional speaking

The world class is known for their attention to detail. Nowhere is this more evident than in their follow up and follow through with people, projects and promises. This is one of the little things separating champions from wannabes. Average people over promise and under deliver. The world class makes big promises and delivers equal or greater results. When a champion tells you they will do something, count on it getting done. Great follow up is one of their habits. Returning telephone calls promptly, writing thank you notes, and connecting people are just a few examples of serious follow up habits. These types of details serve to inspire confidence. Other people of influence confidently recommend the champions to others, and much of this trust is developed through the constant experience of the champions doing what they said they would do. Follow through inspires confidence and fosters trust, and the great ones know it. Average people follow through when they feel like it; the world class follows through regardless of whether they feel like it or not. The great ones are masters of their emotions, and their follow up and follow through habits are a prime example of this valuable skill.

▶ **ACTION STEP FOR TODAY**

Ask this critical thinking question: "How often do I do what I say I am going to do?" Do you follow through every time, or only when you feel like it? Make a commitment to only make promises you can deliver.

164

Champions Do What's Right

"Start with what's right, rather than what is acceptable."
– Peter Drucker, author and management consultant

The world class tends to live by a code of ethics that says, "Do what's right." Since the masses tend to operate from a fear- and scarcity-based consciousness, they are more prone to take unethical shortcuts. They're not bad people; they're frightened people, and frightened people are prone to errors in judgement. On the other hand, champions are operating from a love- and abundance-based consciousness. They believe there is an unlimited source of supply, and they have access to the source. The world class tends to be people of great faith, in one form or another. The common denominator is their faith in themselves and their ability to create the life they've chosen. They trust themselves, and they tend to trust others. This solid mental foundation leads them to do what they believe is right and fair in all their interactions with others. While the middle-class thinker looks to the outside world for answers, world-class thinkers look inside themselves. The great ones have a strong internal frame of reference, and they treat people as they would like to be treated. It has been said the greatest among us answer to a higher calling, and that personifies the champion. The higher calling may come from inside them, or from a higher power, depending on their belief structure. Wherever it comes from, it guides the great ones to do what's right, even if it's unpopular.

▶ **ACTION STEP FOR TODAY**

When you're making decisions that demand ethical consideration, ask this question: "What is the right thing to do?" Follow your higher self and do it, even if it's unusual or unpopular.

165

The Great Ones Think Big

> "The life each of us lives is the life within the limits
> of our own thinking. To have life more abundant, we
> must think in limitless terms of abundance."
>
> *– Thomas Dreier, author*

While average performers think about how to survive with the least amount of pain and struggle, the world class thinks big and plans their brilliant futures. Ask people around you what they think about at any given time, and you might be surprised to learn how many think about just getting by. The world class refers to this as "selling yourself short." Their philosophy seems to be, "If you're going to be thinking, you may as well think big." Their love- and abundance-based consciousness is the engine that drives their big thoughts and creative ideas. The great ones are fearless and focused on manifesting their ultimate dreams. While the middle class thinks about how to avoid pain, the world class thinks about how to gain gratification. One group views the world as a scary place, and the other sees it as an exciting adventure with endless possibilities. The masses see life as a threat; the great ones see it as a game. The difference in thinking is so dramatic between these two groups that, when you talk to them, it's as though you're speaking to people from different planets. The champions' abundance-based consciousness drives them to think and dream bigger with each passing success.

▶ ACTION STEP FOR TODAY

Review your vision for your life, and think about your greatest dreams. Are you selling yourself short? Are you thinking too small? Are you letting fear hold you back from the abundance of life? Do you really have what it takes to hit it big? (Hint: yes!) Rewrite your vision today and go bigger than ever. Trust in your ability to find a way to make your dream come true. You can do it!

▶▶I WORLD-CLASS RESOURCE

Do yourself a favor and pick up The Magic of Thinking Big, by David J. Schwartz. I read it in 1984 and it changed my life.

166

Champions Build Cocoons

*"Champions isolate themselves from the masses,
not out of pretension, but out of practicality.
They know consciousness is contagious."*

– Steve Siebold

One of the things champions are famous for is their ability to build cocoons to protect their thought processes from the disease known as lack consciousness. In short, champions only hang out with other champions. While the middle class judges this as pretentious and elitist, the great ones believe it's essential to their success. Champions believe consciousness is contagious, and know they will become the average of their closest friends and associates. The great ones aren't gamblers. They prefer to be the house. Part of that philosophy is surrounding themselves with people of equal or greater consciousness. The great ones know they don't have the luxury of thinking negative thought. They know one fear-based thought has the power to suffocate a life-changing idea in its infancy. The cocoon protects their consciousness from the onslaught of fear and scarcity. In addition to surrounding themselves with other champions, the world class reads and listens to inspiring books and recordings. Many invest time in spiritual development to strengthen their faith. They attend seminars and workshops to increase their level of awareness and network with other champions, and they also give back to their communities and involve themselves with people who are leaders and activists. In essence, the world class creates an environment firmly entrenched in prosperity consciousness that serves as the rich soil necessary for them to manifest their ultimate vision.

▶ ACTION STEP FOR TODAY

Keeping in mind that consciousness is contagious, and that the people around you can either help you expand your thinking or inject fear and scarcity into your soul, list the people in your inner circle. Is it time to upgrade your cocoon?

COCOONING

Friends and Associates

Listening To Tapes/CDs By Sucessful Authors, Speakers, Philosophers

Reading World-Class Books and Publications

Listening To World-Class Programming CDs

Watching UpliftingTelevision and Movies

Positive vs. Negative Entertainment

Living Conditions,Surrounding Yourself in a Climate of Abundance

▶▶I WORLD-CLASS RESOURCE

Pick up The Dynamic Laws of Prosperity, by Catherine Ponder. Read this book with a highlighter in hand. It's a classic.

167

The World Class Chooses
Repentance Over Blame

"It is important to admit your mistakes, and do
so before you are charged with them. I seize the
earliest opportunity to assume the blame."
– *David Ogilvy, 1911-1999, co-founder,
Ogilvy & Mather Advertising*

A devastating trait of the middle class is their tendency to blame other people, circumstances and events for their shortcomings. While average performers avoid responsibility for their failures, the world class tends to repent. The heart of the champion's consciousness is the belief that all of us are responsible for our own successes, failures and errors in judgment. With this level of conviction, the great ones usually choose to repent, as opposed to making excuses or blaming others. They are the first to apologize and the last to lash out. Many times they take responsibility for breakdowns or failures not directly related to their own actions. This behavior stems from the belief that their elevated level of awareness makes them responsible for watching out for others who are less aware. It's the parent taking responsibility for the child's behavior. While average performers are too busy protecting their egos, the world class operates from a spirit-based consciousness. This gives them the power to change their minds and beliefs if a more accurate truth is realized, without their ego getting in the way. The great ones have evolved enough to recognize the damage their ego can inflict in any given situation. While most champions possess a very healthy ego, they use it to fuel their ambitions, not govern their behavior. In other words, when it comes to interacting with people and problem solving, they bypass their egos and tap their spirits. When champions are wrong, they repent, take responsibility and apologize. This spirit-based consciousness creates an emotional connection with people and fosters more harmonious relationships.

▶ **ACTION STEP FOR TODAY**

Think of an event, circumstance, or behavior for which you were responsible, yet chose not to admit fault and repent. As an experiment, go to the other people involved and apologize. See what happens. Notice how their attitude shifts from ego to spirit, and the level of connection you create as a result. Is this spirit coming from inside the person, or from outside, by way of a higher power? Wherever you believe this spirit originates, the power of repentance cannot be overstated.

168

The Great Ones Grow Up

"People mired in adolescence have no way of knowing that the best is yet to come; it is just past the point where you take responsibility for yourself and your relationships, and leave your self-pity behind. Adulthood has been vastly underrated."

– Dr. Frank Pittman, psychiatrist

While the masses are still wallowing in the past and wondering why things couldn't have been better, the world class grows up and gets on with the great game of life. Most people have never outgrown their adolescence when it comes to controlling their emotions. They are still feeling sorry for themselves and being heavily influenced by the people around them. Fear is an example of this extended adolescence. Children are afraid of many things that pose no actual threat to their well being, such as monsters under the bed or in the closet. The adult masses have the same irrational, made-up fears of events that pose no actual threat, yet hold them back from becoming champions. The fear of rejection, the fear of public speaking, and the fear of success are three examples. When we allow ourselves to buy into these adolescent fears, we are in essence, behaving like children. Champions know that growing up emotionally is essential to achieving world-class results. The great ones still feel fear, but choose to confront their fears and ask themselves if the threat is real or imagined. This critical thinking skill enables the champion to move past many of the obstacles that stop the middle class before they even get started. Many broken marriages are a result of adolescent expectations. The amateur thinker enters the relationship believing their partner has no faults. As times passes and these faults are revealed, the amateur wants to end the relationship and find someone with fewer faults. The pros are grown up enough to know that all of us are fallible human beings with multiple strengths and weaknesses, and that the successful integration of two lives under one roof takes dedication and work. Professional performers grow up and discover that nothing good comes easy, and if it did, we probably wouldn't appreciate its true value. The great ones expect to fight for what they want, so when they hit the inevitable obstacles along the way, they are neither surprised nor intimidated. It all begins with their decision to grow up.

▶ ACTION STEP FOR TODAY

Examine the areas of your life and ask yourself this question: " Am I behaving like an adult in this area...or like a child?"

169

Champions Embrace Diversity

"Diversity is a competitive advantage. Different people approach similar problems in different ways."

– Rich McGinn, CEO, Lucent Technologies

The world class has abandoned any notion or belief that one race, creed or color is any better then the next. They openly embrace ideas and consider ideology from people of different generations, cultures, and philosophies, knowing that every one of us has something to contribute. While amateur thinkers can be quick to judge a book by its cover, the great ones see beyond the package and into the soul. The difference can be summed up by the level of consciousness under which each group operates. With fear and scarcity at the helm, the masses have a sneaking suspicion that anyone different from them is a threat to their security. Since fear breeds fear, the only way the problem can be solved is to abandon this consciousness altogether and ascend to thoughts of love and abundance. This is where the world class resides. They embrace diversity, because they are filled with a spirit-based thought process that is devoid of ego, pretense and fear. Simply stated, the world looks very different when viewed though the eyes of love.

▶ **ACTION STEP FOR TODAY**

Set a goal to make a new friend or business contact of a different race, political affiliation, sexual preference, culture, religion or philosophy. Make a commitment to do this at least once a quarter, and you'll be delighted at the insights you'll gain from a group you may have previously misunderstood.

170

The Great Ones Use
World-Class Language

"Language is the picture and counterpart of thought."
– *Mark Hopkins, author*

The fastest way to identify a person's level of consciousness is by listening to the way they use language. Big words and fancy phrasing don't mean much. As a matter of fact, it can hinder your ability to communicate effectively. When I say "use language," I mean what you say and how you say it. A champion distinguishes himself by the attitude his words convey. You can spot a world-class thinker by listening to his ordinary conversation. A champion is optimistic, future-oriented and confident, and their words and enthusiasm reflect this thought process. While a middle-class thinker talks about "just getting by" and "working for the weekend," a champion uses words such as "thrive" and "prosperity" and "love". The language you use tells the world how you think and serves to reprogram and strengthen your belief in what you say. An average thinker can program himself for abundance as easily as he can program himself for mediocrity! The universe doesn't care; it must give you what you ask for by natural law. So in essence, you either talk yourself into abundance or into scarcity . . . by choice. Most of the world-class performers I've coached or competed with were unaware of this initially, yet, at some point in their lives, learned the truth. Through self-education, they learned the power of programming through language. Thousands have said this one idea contributed more to their success than anything else. They now know they can talk themselves into any reality they desire. The lower levels of consciousness speak the language of fear and scarcity. The great ones speak the language of love and abundance.

▶ **ACTION STEP FOR TODAY**

Become hyper-aware of how people around you talk. Listen to the words they use to describe their experiences. Based on this, evaluate their level of consciousness. Begin to monitor your language, and ask yourself the same question. You're going to be shocked by how easy it is to recognize middle-class consciousness, and how simple it is to upgrade to the world class. The secret is becoming more aware.

▶▶▎ **WORLD-CLASS RESOURCE**

Invest in Power Linguistics, by Dave Yoho.
Visit www.daveyoho.com

171

Champions Understand Cause And Effect

"Society constantly expends its efforts to correct effects rather than causes, which is one reason why the development of human consciousness proceeds so slowly."
– Dr. David Hawkins, M.D., Ph.D, author

The masses tend to focus on effects, rather than on the causes that create the effects. The world class goes directly for the cause and lets the effects take care of themselves. This is most evident in the area of weight loss. America is the fattest country in the world, with more than 65% of our population overweight and 27% are obese. This effect is leading many Americans down the road to diabetes, heart disease and death. So how do the masses solve the problem? They swallow pills, go on crash diets, and starve themselves until they can no longer stand it. All these methods treat the effects. They're an external solution to an internal problem. The cause is the way people think about food and exercise, and the solution is to change those thoughts. When those thoughts are upgraded from middle class to world class, the weight problem gently fades and never returns. The internal problem is solved with an internal solution. Our level of health and fitness, like everything else in our lives, is the direct manifestation of how we think. It's the outward appearance of our internal thoughts. Average thinkers are unaware of this truth, and would most likely reject it as being too pedestrian to work even if they were made aware of it. Like most of the secrets of the world class, it's simple and straightforward. Cause and effect are no different, yet the great ones go from knowing this to actually using it. That's one of the reasons we call them champions.

▶ **ACTION STEP FOR TODAY**

Look at the major areas of your life and ask what's holding you back from getting better. Next, identify the causes that are creating the effects, and set a goal to attack the cause and solve the problem.

172

The World Class Relies On Infinite Intelligence

"Religion is about obedience. Spirituality is about self-discovery."
— *Bill Gove, 1912-2001, the father of professional speaking*

The world class's spirit-driven consciousness is one of the biggest advantages they have in business and in life. Champions are not ashamed to ask for help, whether it comes in the form of a mentor or someplace higher. One of the ancient secrets of the great ones is asking for guidance and wisdom from a higher power. Secularists call it meditation; the spiritual call it prayer. Secularists believe the wisdom meditation offers comes from inside the subconscious mind. The spiritual believe their wisdom comes from God. Some people believe it taps into both. Whatever their individual belief, the great ones believe in a source of infinite intelligence upon which they can draw. Champions know the secret to connecting to a higher plane is tuning into the vibrational frequency of the source. This begins by quieting the mind. The secularists seek out a quiet place; the spiritual often go to church or a chapel. The goal is to create sufficient space between their thoughts in order to gain perspective and begin thinking on a higher frequency.

▶ ACTION STEP FOR TODAY

Ask this critical thinking question: "Do I use meditation or prayer as a means of gaining wisdom?" If yes, the next question is, "Am I meditating or praying out of love or fear?"

▶▶I WORLD-CLASS RESOURCE

There's a Spiritual Solution to Every Problem, by Dr. Wayne Dyer.

173

The Great Ones Manifest Energy

"The real difference between men is energy. A strong will, a settled purpose, an invincible determination, can accomplish almost anything; and in this lies the distinction between great men and little men."

— Thomas Fuller, 1710-1790, African slave and mathematician

The engine behind every great champion's success is energy in three forms: physical, mental and spiritual. Because the world class operates from a love- and abundance-based consciousness, they appear to have almost boundless energy. At a lower level, the masses operate from fear – the biggest energy sucker known to man. Love attracts energy; fear consumes it. Is it any wonder average people are tired and worn out half the time? The masses unconsciously deplete their own energy. Champions create energy through their thoughts, and their thoughts produce feelings that reinforce their belief that everything happens for a reason. The great ones believe they are destiny's darlings; that they were born to win. No matter how bad things get, they believe the universe is conspiring to help them. This belief in universal favor becomes a self-fulfilling prophecy and attracts all three forms of energy. This pattern creates a psychological tidal wave of momentum that drives performers beyond normal limits of energy. In contrast, middle-class performers think thoughts and manifest feelings rooted in fear, which drains energy and attracts additional fear. The masses suffer physical, mental and spiritual fatigue from their own thought processes. They are the architects of their own destruction, even though they are completely capable of redesigning their consciousness. By natural law, energy is created or consumed by thought, and the great ones choose to create it.

▶ **ACTION STEP FOR TODAY**

Be aware of the thoughts you have and ask yourself if they are creating or consuming energy. Just for today, allow only energy-generating thoughts to occupy your mind. Notice the physical, mental and spiritual impact it has on you.

▶▶| **WORLD-CLASS RESOURCE**

For further study, pick up a copy of Power vs. Force, by David R. Hawkins, M.D., Ph.D. This book is 300 pages of solid research, guaranteed to stir the deepest parts of your imagination. You may never see human behavior the same way again.

174
Champions Embrace Nonlinear Thinking

"Nonlinear thinking is the manifestation of a performer's flaming desire to breathe life into his or her ultimate vision."
— Steve Siebold

Nonlinear thinking has been referred to as "thinking out of the box." The root of this thought process has more to do with philosophy than strategy. When the middle class says, "it's impossible," the world class agrees. Then they say, "but if it were possible, how would it be done?" This is why professional performers are the ones who solve society's most complex problems. The masses believe problem solving stems from knowledge. The great ones believe it stems from will. Once they have established the will to succeed, there is no turning back. Their incredible determination creates the need for nonlinear thinking, combined with boundless energy. Champions also earn money in nonlinear ways. While the masses essentially trade their time for money, the great ones realize this is probably the worst way to acquire wealth. Using nonlinear tools such as compound interest, employees, network marketing, joint ventures, strategic alliances, and others, they build wealth by creating leverage. The upper class, classified as wealthy in financial terms, generates their money primarily by their job or business. The world class, often classified as super-rich in financial terms, generates their money primarily through investments. The bigger the champion, the more they use leverage as a tool in all areas of life, and it all starts with a nonlinear thought process.

▶ **ACTION STEP FOR TODAY**
Examine your problem-solving thought processes. Notice whether you're thinking in linear or nonlinear terms. Take a second look at your biggest problems. Is it possible to take a nonlinear approach to solving them?

175

The World Class Gets Paid To Think

"Creative thinking is today's most prized, profit-producing possession for any individual, corporation or country. It has the capacity to change you, your business and the world."
– *Robert P. Crawford, author*

Today, the highest-paying position in business is the professional thinker, and the world class knows it. While amateur thinkers continue to follow the old-world philosophy of "hard work is the key to success," champions have evolved over the years from working harder, to working smarter, to critical thinking. The age of the mind has caused confusion among the masses because of its nonlinear nature. Creative thought flourishes in a mental climate of peace, quiet, and harmony, and cannot be coaxed or coerced. Any attempt to force it produces congestion and stifles the neurological network. The secret to world-class thinking is circulation, and the key to circulation is letting go. The great ones never attempt to control or force thoughts; they simply create a climate in which creative thought can flourish and grow. The masses will tell you the corporate CEOs and other executives are overpaid, because they think in linear terms. Average people are still dividing the executives' salary by the number of hours they spend at the office. That's why the masses believe the world class is overpaid. In truth, most executives are underpaid, considering they spend nearly every waking minute thinking about how to help their companies grow and prosper. When average people go home after forty or fifty hours of work, executives are almost always still on the job. They may not be in the office, but the office is on their mind. The days of using physical strength to prosper are over. From this point forward, the world belongs to the men and women of the mind.

▶ **ACTION STEP FOR TODAY**

List five ways you can increase your value to your business or career by creating new ideas.

▶▶I **WORLD-CLASS RESOURCE**

Read How Rich People Think,
howrichpeoplethinkbook.com

176

The Good And Great Are Separated By A Razor's Edge

"Desire plus sacrifice plus discipline equals preparation. Preparation plus success equals confidence. Mental toughness plus pride equals perseverance. If you have confidence and persevere, you will always have the edge. If you have the edge, you will succeed. Eventually."

– Howard Ferguson, 1938-1989, wrestling coach, author

Average people tend to believe world-class performers are so superior, so far out in front, so much smarter and more talented that there is absolutely no way they could become one – and it's not true. It's not even close. The truth, as the evidence in this book suggests, is there is really only a razor's edge separating the good from the great, or the middle class from the world class. Granted, it's a razor's edge in many different areas, a series of critical subtleties that makes all the difference. The real question this book presents to middle-class performers is this: is it possible for a person of average intelligence and modest means to ascend to the throne of the world class? The answer is an enthusiastic YES! Of course it's possible. The question is not one of possibility, but of will. History has shown us the majority of people will not rise up and take the challenge. They could – they have the intelligence and the potential – yet they won't. It's not because they lack desire, but because they don't believe it's possible. They are tired of being disappointed. It's easier to simply turn on the television, or engage in some other mind-numbing activity. Could they alter their level of expectation and forge ahead? You bet! Through language change and visualization, they could artificially manufacture a higher level of expectation, regardless of where they are now. Again, the statistics say most will never even attempt it. When you go pro, it's much easier to compete against amateurs. At the risk of sounding preachy, I have been both an amateur and a pro, and I highly recommend going pro. Emotionally and mentally, it's actually much more comfortable after you cross the barrier. How do you go pro? It's simple. You decide to do it. Period. Then just go back through this book with a highlighter and model the thought processes, habits, and philosophies of the great ones.

▶ ACTION STEP FOR TODAY

Conduct a critical analysis of yourself as a performer. Rate yourself on a scale of 1 to 7, 7 being highest, in terms of the following habits: sacrifice, discipline, confidence, pride, and mental toughness. If you scored less than 7 in any area, make a commitment to do further study on this habit. Any change or improvement in any of these habits has the power to rocket your results.

▶▶ WORLD-CLASS RESOURCE

Get a copy of the late Howard Ferguson's classic, The Edge: The Guide to Fulfilling Dreams, Maximizing Success and Enjoying a Lifetime of Achievement. This book has become a collector's item for top performers everywhere. It's loaded with quotations and philosophies of many of the world's most outstanding athletes.

177

School Is Never Out For The Great Ones

"The A students work for the B students, the B students work for the C students, and the D students dedicate the buildings. The most successful among us are not always the class valedictorians, but they are the best self-educated people on the planet."

— Unknown

Twenty years ago, why some people were so much more successful and fulfilled than others was a mystery to me. Were they smarter? More educated? More talented? The answer is no. Oh, I've come across a genius or two over the years, but 99% of the time, the answer is much simpler. The great ones become great because they are more mentally tough. Through time and effort, they have learned to take control of their thoughts, feelings and attitudes in the game of life and in turn, life has rewarded them handsomely. You can do the same thing if you'll commit yourself to never ending personal growth and development. I've said this many times throughout this book, but it's worthy of repeating: Champions invest time in getting better. School is never out for the great ones. Have you ever been to the bookstore and wondered who reads all those business and self-improvement books? It's not the poverty class, or the working class, or the middle class. It's the world class. The people who need it most wouldn't even consider it, and the people who need it least wouldn't consider missing it. A never-ending cycle of self-education is the centerpiece of world-class consciousness. All it takes to get started is a decision to do it. Throughout this book, I've referenced the old cliché, "The rich get richer and the poor get poorer." When I first began studying mental toughness, I didn't understand why. I do now. After reading this book, I hope you do, too.

▶ **ACTION STEP FOR TODAY**

Ask yourself these critical thinking questions:

      1) Am I really committed to going pro?

      2) Am I willing to do whatever it takes to fulfill my vision?

      3) Am I willing to put a plan together to implement the suggestions in ....this book?

Learning Resources

- *How Rich People Think*
  www.howrichpeoplethinkbook.com

- *177 Mental Toughness Secrets - CD Album*
  www.mentaltoughnesssecrets.com

- *Coaching 177 Mental Toughness Secrets*
  www.coachingmentaltoughness.com

- *Mental Toughness Blog*
  www.MentalToughnessBlog.com

- *Mental Toughness University*
  www.mentaltoughnessuniversity.com

- *Mental Toughness College*
  www.mentaltoughnesscollege.com

- *Mental Toughness Mastery*
  www.mentaltoughnessmastery.com

- *The Making of a Million Dollar Mind*
  www.milliondollarmind.com

- *Fatloser - Mental Toughness for Weight Control*
  www.fatloser.com

- *Die Fat or Get Tough*
  www.diefatbook.com

- *Speaker Steve Siebold*
  www.speakerstevesiebold.com

- *Bill Gove Speech Workshop*
  www.feepaidprofessionalspeaker.com

- *Public Speakers Blog*
  www.publicspeakersblog.com

- *Free Speaking Course*
  www.freespeakingcourse.com

Do You Think Like a Millionaire?

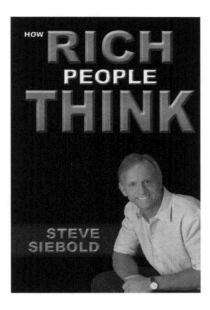

This book will teach you how. It compares the thoughts, habits and philosophies of the middle class to the world class when it comes to wealth. The differes are as extreme as they are numerous. The strategy is simple: learn how rich people think, copy them, take action and get rich This book will teach you how. It compares the thoughts, habits and philosophies of the middle class to the world class when it comes to wealth. The strategy is simple: learn how rich people think, copy them, take action and get rich. If you've ever dreamed of living a life most people only see in movies, study this book like a scientist. Freedom from financial worries and a millionaire's lifestyle is closer than you think.

**How Rich People Think has been featured on
ABC, NBC, CBS, CNBC and the Fox Business Network.**

GET 5 CHAPTERS FOR FREE AT
www.HowRichPeopleThinkBook.com

Mental Toughness University
Helps Companies Increase Sales And Move Market Share By Creating A No Excuses-High Performance Culture

Mental Toughness University is a comprehensive mental training process that moves sales and management teams from good to great. Mental Toughness trains people how to control their thoughts, feelings, and attitudes, before, during and after a performance. Especially under pressure.

What Are The Benefits of Mental Toughness Training?

Most MTU corporate clients are sales and management teams that report dramatic increases in sales. Management teams benefit by learning how to coach the mental toughness process and implement it immediately into their daily coaching with their sales team. Managers often adopt new criteria for hiring salespeople after completing the course. Employee retention rates are also affected due to the personal benefits gained during the training. MTU delivers both professional and personal results. Since most research shows that an employee's job is not the most important aspect of his or her life, the ongoing personal benefits of this program tend to raise the switching cost of an employee moving to another company. Companies often experience enhanced customer service from the participants as a result of their new level of focus on the customer.

Mental Toughness University is Not a Traditional Training Program.
MTU is a Process, Not a Program.

It's about training people how to THINK like world-class performers, and how to control and manipulate their own emotions for MAXIMUM performance. MTU is a cross between emotional intelligence training and critical thinking. It's an introspective process that causes people to examine their thoughts, feelings attitudes, and beliefs and how they are directly impacting their results. We call the process, 'Facilitated Introspection'. The six-hour program is an awakening to expose participants to the process and show them there's a higher level of emotional competence and mental performance than they are experiencing. MTU facilitates this emotional transformation over the next 12 months during the teleconference follow up program. Each participant is assigned 20 minutes of homework each week and held accountable for submitting it. Both the six-hour seminar and the follow-up teleconferences are highly interactive. Most people that go through the process have never been exposed to this level of personal introspection. They may be familiar with some of the content, but the real growth and change comes from them getting to know themselves. Most participants are shocked and surprised to learn how little they know about themselves. The Mental Toughness University Process has the power to bring out the best in any performer who will engage his or her mind in the process.

For more information, visit www.mentaltoughnessuniversity.com

MENTAL TOUGHNESS MASTERY
12 CD Series

The great ones believe that nearly any goal is within their reach, and this single belief sets off a mental domino effect that continues to manifest one success after another. They literally THINK their way to the top, and 99% of them are no smarter than you and I.

Here's the problem:
It's not easy to make the distinction between the good and the great unless you know what you're looking for. After 20 years of studying champions, I've discovered that it's really a series of subtleties that add up to make the difference. Without knowing what to look for, most people will completely miss these subtleties. When you stand the champion next to a middle-class performer, there doesn't appear to be much difference. Have you ever thought to yourself, "I can't figure out why so and so is so successful; he/she doesn't seem to be any different than me or anyone else?"

Me, too. But not anymore. The differences are huge, but not very visible. So here's what I've done. I've selected the biggest differences between the winners and the still-trying, and I've put all of this information on a 12 CD series called Mental Toughness Mastery. You will receive 12 CDs detailing exactly how champions think and process information, as well as real life stories and examples of the world-class performers I've worked with over the years, and how to incorporate these ideas and philosophies into your life . . . immediately.

Order by calling 561.733.9078 or visit
www.mentaltoughnessmastery.com

The Making Of A
Million Dollar Mind

"Have You Got What It Takes To Produce

Million Dollar Results?"

For most people, the answer is YES and NO.

YES, they have the POTENTIAL and TALENT.

NO, they lack the BELIEF SYSTEM it takes to ACHIEVE
and SUSTAIN World Class Results.

It's sad, but true.

That's why you see people who have won the lottery losing it,
or getting in trouble with the IRS, or plagued with other self-induced difficulties.

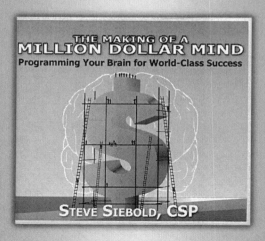

For the top ten distinctions between middle class and world class thinkers visit
www.milliondollarmind.com

Mental Toughness for Dieters

FREE 21 DAY FAT LOSER PROGRAM

FatLoser.com is Mental Toughness Training for Dieters, Coached by World-Renowned Expert STEVE SIEBOLD, featured on The Today Show, Good Morning America and CNN World News

PLAY VIDEO

INTRODUCTION

Register for this FREE 21-day video coaching course and lose weight now!

Register for this FREE 21-day video coaching course and lose weight now!

Each day for the next 21 days you'll receive an email with a link to your 10-15 minute training video for the day. After you watch the video answer three short questions about how you're feeling about your progress. After 21-days of Mental Toughness Training for weight loss, you'll have the tools you need to go the distance and create the body you desire and deserve. Watch the introduction video above, register for the FREE course and get started now! Your new body and your new life are waiting!

visit www.fatloser.com

Study The World's Highest Paid Skill: Public Speaking

The # 1 Professional Public Speakers Video Blog

HOME   STEVE SIEBOLD

SPEAKING ON NATIONAL TELEVISION
By steve

One of the fastest ways to catapult your public speaking career is to be interviewed on national television. Last year I was on the Today Show, Good Morning America, FOX, ABC News, NBC, CBS, and a bunch of others. I can tell you from experience this is one the best things you can do for your career. In this short 3-minute video post, I share some of the most important tips for succeeding in this medium.

SPEAKING IN STADIUMS
By steve

One of the greatest thrills you can have as a professional speaker is addressing a sold-out stadium packed with 10,000 people. In 40-minutes you can reach more people with your message than most speakers reach in years. I've been lucky enough to give lots of stadium speeches, and I've learned some important lessons along the way. Speaking in a stadium is different than speaking to 100, 500, or even 1,000 people. There are many more variables to consider and far more things that can go wrong. In this short video, I'll give you three of the most important differences you want to be prepared for.

WHAT IS YOUR PUBLIC SPEAKING DREAM?
By steve

Subscribe Today for FREE at

www.PublicSpeakersBlog.com

Are you interested in building a million-dollar speaking career?

Course Details

This 10-day course is designed to give you an insider's overview of the professional speaking business and teach you how to build a million-dollar speaking career. Over the course of 10-days, you'll have access to one short 10-15 minute video per day, complete with questions to answer that will help you create a customized speaking business tailored to your expertise, interests, and financial goals.

You Will Learn...

- ✓ How to select your topic
- ✓ How to build a multi-dimensional business model
- ✓ How to become a personality speaker
- ✓ How to break into the two major speaking markets
- ✓ How to leverage the power of your keynote speech
- ✓ How to become a niche market celebrity
- ✓ How to build your referral network
- ✓ How to become an profitable author
- ✓ How to sell yourself as a professional speaker
        ...And much more

Each day you will watch a short video and answer homework questions. Upon successful completion of this course, you will receive an official certificate of achievement. As a graduate, you will know more about the inner-workings of the professional speaking business than most professional speakers. No kidding. Here's why: Your coach for the 10-day course is Steve Siebold, CSP. Steve Siebold ranks among the top 1% of income earners worldwide in the professional speaking industry. Siebold was the protégé of the late Bill Gove, the father of the professional speaking industry, and one of the most successful keynote speakers of all-time. After attending the Bill Gove Speech Workshop in 1996, and spending five years on the road speaking with Mr. Gove, Steve Siebold rocketed to the top tier of the speaking industry and became a million-dollar professional speaker. Steve Siebold will give you insights into the speaking business that only a handful of speakers in the business fully understand, and how you can use them to live your dreams as a fee-paid professional speaker.

You get all of this for FREE. No catch. No strings. Your new career is waiting for you.

Register at www.FreeSpeakingcourse.com today!

About The Author

Steve Siebold is a former professional athlete and national coach. He's spent the past 26 years studying the thought processes, habits and philosophies of world-class performers. Today he helps Fortune 500 companies increase sales through mental toughness training. His clients include Johnson & Johnson, Toyota, and Procter & Gamble. His national television show: *Mental Toughness* with Steve Siebold, won the 2007 Telly Award for best motivational show. Steve has appeared on The Today Show, Good Morning America, ABC News, FOX Television, CBS, TBS, BBC in Europe, NBC Australia and dozens of others. As a professional speaker, Steve ranks among the top 1% of income earners worldwide. Steve's blog, www.mentaltoughnessblog.com, is one of the fastest growing personal development video blogs on the Internet, with thousands of subscribers around the globe.

Steve has been married since 1986 to Dawn Andrews. The couple spends summers on Lake Lanier in North Georgia, and winters in Palm Beach County, Florida.

Made in the USA
San Bernardino, CA
11 December 2015